Greater Spokane and Palouse Region Back Roads Cycling Guide

Forty Bike Trips on the Back Roads of Stevens, Pend Oreille, Spokane, Whitman, Lincoln, Adams and Franklin Counties

David R. Heflick

Silcox Productions, Orient, Washington

Greater Spokane and Palouse Region Back Roads Cycling Guide

Forty Bike Trips on the Back Roads of Stevens, Pend Oreille, Spokane, Whitman, Lincoln, Adams and Franklin Counties

By David R. Heflick

Published by: Silcox Productions
P.O. Box 1407
Orient WA 99160
(509) 684-8287
dheflick@plix.com

ISBN: 0-9638705-6-4 (soft cover)
Library of Congress Catalog Card Number: 98-90215

Cover design by Tim Kaage, Laurel Graphx

Cover artwork by Tim Kaczorowski, Paramark Design

Printed in Canada by Hignell Book Printing

Through the hills, valleys, forests, coulees, and wheat fields,
there is one who forever rides with you.

In memory of Cooper O'Neil Jones (April 16, 1984 - July 2, 1997)

Acknowledgments

Several people provided data and resources that contributed significantly to the information presented in this book. Specifically, I wish to thank Phil Barto, Margaret Watson, and Andrew Worlock for assistance with the Spokane Area map. A big thanks to Eileen Hyatt for the chapter on bicycle safety. In addition, thanks to Gordon Savatsky for a pre-publication review and Cynthia Tierney for countless hours of proof reading.

Contents

Introductory Chapters

Trip Descriptions

Touring the Region

Resources

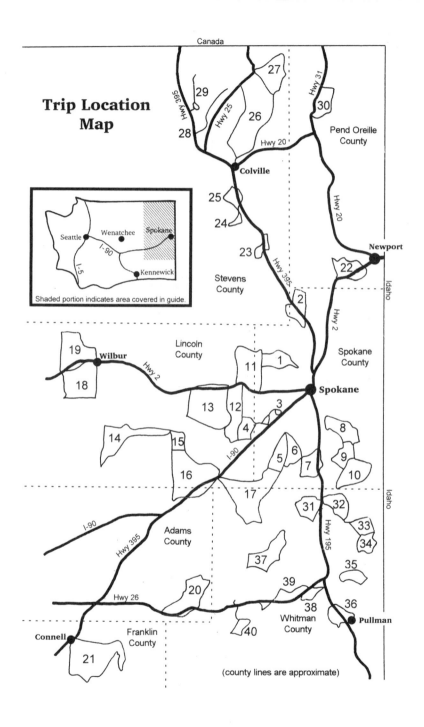

Trip Location Map

Shaded portion indicates area covered in guide.

Seattle • Wenatchee • Spokane • Kennewick • I-90 I-5

Canada

Colville

Newport

Wilbur

Spokane

Connell

Pullman

Hwy 395
Hwy 25
Hwy 31
Hwy 20
Hwy 2
Hwy 195
Hwy 26
I-90

Pend Oreille County

Stevens County

Lincoln County

Spokane County

Adams County

Franklin County

Whitman County

Idaho

(county lines are approximate)

Trip List

Spokane County

1: Sontag Park - Four Mound Prairie
2: Deer Park - Williams Valley
3: Medical Lake - Silver Lake
4: Medical Lake - Bennett Meadow - Tucker Prairie
5: Cheney - Turnbull Wildlife Refuge (Loop 1)
6: Cheney - Turnbull Wildlife Refuge (Loop 2)
7: Spangle - Plaza
8: Rockford - Hangman Valley
9: Rockford - Waverly
10: Fairfield - Tekoa Mountain - Waverly

Lincoln, Adams & Franklin Counties

11: Reardan - Spring Creek Canyon - Devil's Gap
12: Reardan - Waukon - Edwall
13: Davenport - Bluestem
14: Harrington - Channeled Scablands - Odessa
15: Harrington - Lord's Valley
16: Sprague - Crab Creek Scablands
17: Sprague - Williams Lake - Ewan
18: Wilbur - Wilson Creek Flood Channel
19: Wilbur North
20: Washtucna - Palouse River - Staley Coulee
21: Connell - Snake River - Devil's Canyon

Pend Oreille & Stevens Counties

22: Scotia Valley - Deer Valley - Sacheen Lake
23: Chewelah - Waitts Lake
24: Addy - Blue Creek
25: Addy - Marble Valley Basin
26: Colville - Northport
27: Northport - Cedar Lake - Deep Lake
28: Columbia River Out-and-Back
29: Barstow - Kettle River - Pierre Lake
30: Ione - Sullivan Lake

Whitman County

31: Rosalia - Pine City - Pine Creek
32: Rosalia - Oakesdale
33: Oakesdale - Farmington
34: Garfield - Farmington
35: Palouse - Eden Valley
36: Albion - Pullman
37: St. John - Palouse Basin - Endicott
38: Colfax - Union Flat Creek Valley
39: Colfax Fairgrounds - Dusty
40: Lacrosse - Hay

1

How to Use This Guide

This book describes 40 bicycle trips—mostly loops—in the eastern third of Washington. It represents a comprehensive survey of the paved back roads of the greater Spokane area, the Palouse region, and the Colville National Forest. Maximum flexibility has been built into each route: short cuts and alternate routes are included in most of the trips, and many loops have adjacent routes.

Trip maps have been designed to highlight the main route, making it easy to see at a glance just where the route will take you. Virtually all intersecting paved roads are shown, as well as campgrounds, lakes, rivers, and other landmarks. Town grids are used to indicate approximate size and city-limit boundaries. Often, in order to show more detail, areas within the grids are not drawn to scale. City streets will generally be closer together than the map indicates.

Road names on trip maps indicate the signed name of a road in cases where the road is actually signed. However, many of eastern Washington's back roads are not signed. When such is the case, you will be advised in the mileage log. Usually, intersecting roads are far enough apart that it is not difficult to stay on course. However, it is a good idea to look ahead in the mileage log for any unsigned roads on the route and take special care not to miss a turn. When there is a discrepancy between the signed name and the name indicated on a county road map, both names are provided. The names of county roads often change when they pass through a town. Every effort has been made to indicate these variations on the trip maps and mileage logs.

Elevation profiles are stretched out to full-page width to give a more detailed representation of each trip's overall elevation gain. However, there are often numerous smaller ups and downs too shallow for representation on the graph, making the cumulative elevation gain of the trip greater than it may appear. Reading the trip descriptions and mileage-log text will help you determine how much, if any, additional climbing you may expect. If *roller coaster hills* are mentioned, plan accordingly for the extra energy requirements.

A cycling altimeter measures minute changes in atmospheric pressure that occur as elevation increases. Because atmospheric pressure at any given elevation varies depending upon weather conditions, the altimeter must be recalibrated before each trip in order to establish a starting-point reading, based upon current atmospheric pressure at a known elevation level. Unfortunately, changing weather conditions during the course of the ride affect the altimeter's ability to measure altitude changes with 100-percent accuracy. For this reason, it is not uncommon for the instrument to show a difference of 100 feet between the starting and ending reading of a bike route that begins and ends at the same location. Therefore, elevation profiles are intended to provide a graphic image of the number and steepness of hills rather than an exact indication of elevation at any given point.

The elevation readings start at zero for each trip and are given in 100-foot increments. The readings are shown on the vertical scale along the left side of the graph. Mileage readings are given in one-mile increments and are shown horizontally along the bottom of the graph. Below the mileage readings, key features of the trip are indicated along with arrows that provide correlating mileage. A vertical arrow is used to pinpoint the location of towns and specific stops along the way. Horizontal arrows are used to indicate the length of passages through valleys, along bodies of water, and similar aspects of the trip.

Insets providing precise specifications on the steepness of significant hills are included in the graphs. The specifications are given in feet per mile. A reading of 200 f/m means that you will gain 200 feet in elevation for every mile you travel. To convert the specifications to grade, divide the specification by 52.8. Using this formula, 200 f/m is equivalent to a 3.78% grade.

What is a steep hill to one cyclist is an easy hill to the next. Your level of fitness, the weight and efficiency of your bike, and your mental attitude are among the factors that contribute to your judgment of a hill's steepness. For the purposes of this book, the following scale was used in determining the terminology for describing hills:

  75 f/m: easy
150 f/m: moderate
250 f/m: fairly steep
330 f/m: steep
400 f/m: very steep

Don't let the elevation profiles intimidate you; limitations imposed by available space on the page cause the hills to look much steeper than they actually are. Reading the feet-per-mile indications on the graphs and using the scale above will help you determine just how challenging those hills are going to be.

Mileage logs indicate cumulative mileage readings at turns, intersections, and landmarks. (While an odometer is not an absolute requirement, it is strongly recommended that you use one.) Keep in mind, however, that differences in odometers, failure to turn your odometer off during side trips, and other variables will quickly lead to a discrepancy between the guide's indications and your odometer readings. It is best to note your mileage at key points and use the guide's indications more for determining the mileage *between* points than an indication of what your odometer ought to read at any given point. Keeping track of intersections and other landmarks will help keep you on course.

Mileage logs have keyed text to make it easier to scan for specific types of information. Text is keyed as follows:

Bold type: indicates an action you must take to stay on course
Bold italics: indicates a warning
Regular italics: indicates water, food, restrooms, etc.
Indented italics: short cut, side trip, or alternate route

Traffic indications are given for most roads. Use these only as a very general guideline. Traffic volumes vary seasonally, especially in recreational areas; the traffic levels you experience on a given trip may differ substantially from those observed when the route was surveyed. Traffic levels near city and residential areas will also vary significantly with the time of day. Always be prepared for potentially higher traffic levels than indicated and stay alert for cars at all times.

A **Spokane city and suburb** map is included in Chapter 4 for residents and visitors to use in finding the best routes in, out, and through the city. Here, you'll also find suggestions for close-in loops and trips, and information on the Centennial Trail.

A **trip selector** map is provided following the Table of Contents to give an overall view of the guide's coverage and to indicate the location of each trip.

A **trip connector** map is located in Chapter 8, indicating various routes to connect the trips for longer tours.

2

Cycling Safety

This chapter was contributed by Eileen Hyatt, who serves both as Education Director for the Spokane Bicycle Club and Effective Cycling Instructor for the League of American Bicyclists. Please see the Appendix for more information on these organizations.

Ride a safe bike. A safe bike is one that fits, is comfortable, and is appropriate for the riding you'll be doing. A good bike shop will help you find the right bicycle, asking questions about your plans and offering bikes, helmets, clothing, and accessories appropriate for your needs at a variety of prices.

A safe bike is a well-maintained bike. While a bike-shop checkup will contribute toward your safety, you must be on the lookout for signs of trouble before and during a ride. Before heading out, check for loose parts and make sure tires and brakes are in good condition.

While single-bike accidents and collisions with other cyclists are the most common type of bike crashes, collisions with automobiles are the most serious. Traffic violations are the biggest cause of such collisions. You must take charge of your own safety. Bicycles are considered vehicles in all fifty states and are safest when cyclists follow the rules of the road. This does not always come naturally to riders who have been cautioned to "stay out of the way of cars." Behaving unpredictably or riding out of sight of motorists is dangerous, irritating behavior. Be predicable to other drivers by following traffic laws:

- ride on the right-hand side of the road or along the right side of the lane that is heading the direction you wish to go

- in addition to checking your mirror, look over your shoulder and make eye contact before making a transition into a left-turn lane

- use hand signals to let others know of your intentions

- obey traffic signs and signals

- equip your bike with lights and reflectors.

Compensate for your smaller size by making sure you are visible to motorists more used to watching for car-sized objects:

- wear bright colors

- use lights when riding at night

- establish eye contact with motorists to be certain they are aware of your presence.

Continually look in all directions for road hazards as you ride. Be aware of traffic conditions behind you before swerving to avoid objects in the roadway. A rearview mirror helps you keep tabs on vehicles approaching from behind.

Wet, rainy conditions require increased caution. Allow extra space for stopping. Railroad tracks and cobblestones are especially slippery when wet. Make yourself more visible on dreary days.

As a general rule, use the front and rear brakes evenly, but ease up on the front brake if the rear wheels skids and when turning on softer, dirt surfaces. Whenever possible, avoid turning or braking on gravel, utility covers, pavement markings, etc.

Cross railroad tracks at a right angle after scanning behind to be sure traffic is clear. Stand up to absorb the shock of tracks and other uneven surfaces.

When riding in groups, ride in a straight line at an even pace. Allow a safe stopping distance between yourself and the the bike ahead. Ride only with cyclists you know to be smooth, experienced, predictable riders. Avoid *group think*—judge traffic situations for yourself. Point out hazards and potentially dangerous situations to other riders in the group. While it is legal to ride two abreast on Washington highways, keep an eye in your mirror and form a single line when traffic approaches from the rear. Pull completely off the roadway when stopping to rest.

Effective Cycling classes are offered in many communities in the U.S. and Canada. Check with your local bicycle club or the League of American Bicyclists.

WEAR A PROPERLY FITTED HELMET EVERY TIME YOU RIDE!

3

Enhancing Cycling Pleasure

For long-distance cycling to be enjoyable, you must achieve good aerobic conditioning, become *saddle conditioned,* eat properly before and during a ride, wear proper clothing, protect yourself from the elements, and equip your bike with appropriate accessories.

Achieving **aerobic fitness** means preparing your cardiovascular system to efficiently distribute the blood and oxygen your body needs under taxing conditions. In order to do this, you must exercise a minimum of three times per week, achieving a *target heart rate* (based on age and gender) for a minimum of 20 minutes. Dr. Kenneth Cooper, the aerobics guru, has written a number of books on the topic, which are available in book stores everywhere.

An area of conditioning often overlooked by the novice cyclist is **saddle conditioning**. No amount of aerobic exercise can prepare you for the long hours of seat-to-seat contact you'll experience on a series of long-distance rides—that is, unless your aerobic exercise is conducted on a bike. Even then you must spend more than 20 minutes a day three times a week on the bike to get your posterior ready for long hours in the saddle. Work your way toward long-distance cycling by riding regularly and gradually increasing distances.

Proper **nutrition** is critical. What you eat before a ride will have an enormous impact on your energy level. In the hours immediately prior to and during a ride, eat foods high in complex carbohydrates—fruits (bananas are the ultimate bike food), bagels, grains, fruit bars, oatmeal and other cereals. Avoid fat- and protein-oriented foods such as meats, eggs, beans, and dairy products. Fat and protein are too slow in digesting and deprive your body of energy in the process. The night before a ride is the time to eat such foods, as they help your body prepare for the next day's ride.

In addition to the proper foods, you'll also need lots of **water** to keep your body hydrated. While individual differences and riding conditions are significant variables, a good rule of thumb for calculating water needs is one quart of water for every hour of cycling.

Proper **clothing** will add considerably to your enjoyment. While specialized cycling clothing is not required, such clothing is specifically designed for ventilation, reduced chaffing, and low wind resistance. Whatever route you decide to go—conventional clothing or specialized cycling wear—bike test all clothing items for comfort and functionality before wearing them on a long trip.

The **elements**—wind, sun, heat, and cold—can take a heavy toll. Be prepared with lip balm, sunscreen, high-quality sunglasses, and foul-weather protection.

Minimal **accessories** include a properly fitted helmet, basic bike tools and the knowledge to use them, water-bottle racks, bell or ringer (particularly for city riding—they are sometimes required), and a rear-view mirror. While not absolutely necessary, an odometer is a tremendous assistance in staying on course. In addition, a seat bag or luggage rack simplifies the packing of food and clothing. A simple, inexpensive, and flexible pack arrangement consists of a small, rectangular kneeling pad (check your local garden center) placed underneath a nylon bag strapped to the rack with lightweight bungie cords (about 1/8" thick and 12" long). The cords can be tied together to span larger bags. The pad will prevent hard items such as tools and keys, which invariably find their way to the bottom of the bag, from rattling against the aluminum rack; it also serves as a sitting pad during rest stops or a kneeling pad when making repairs or adjustments.

One last thing: if you'll be regularly transporting your bike by automobile, work out a system for doing so. Nothing will discourage you faster than a big hassle every time you have to load or unload. There is a style of bike rack for virtually every vehicle and taste. If you have a larger vehicle, you can get along without a rack. With smaller station wagons, removing the front wheel, lowering or removing the seat, and lowering the handle bars make it possible to roll a bike, rear first, into the vehicle. Even without quick-release components, this can be done in a matter of minutes if you're organized. Purchase the needed tools (and a small shop towel for wiping your hands) and leave them in the vehicle, reserving their use solely for the purpose of bike assembly and disassembly.

Zen and the art of harvesting (trip 8, Valley-Chapel Road)

Rolling down to the base of Tekoa Mountain (trip 10)

4

Spokane County

The city of Spokane is the dominant feature of Spokane County. While the roads within and immediately surrounding the city itself are too heavily traveled to lend themselves to genuine back-roads cycling, there are some fine routes only a few miles outside the city limits, including trips through the Turnbull Wildlife Refuge, Hangman Valley, Indian Prairie, Tucker Prairie, and Williams Valley. In addition, you'll find trips through multi-colored wheat fields that roll right up to the mountains across the Idaho border.

Following the back-roads route descriptions are bike-route maps of Spokane, the Centennial Trail, and suggested loops in the areas immediately outside the city limits.

Trips:

    1: Sontag Park - Four Mound Prairie
    2: Deer Park - Williams Valley
    3: Medical Lake - Silver Lake
    4: Medical Lake - Bennett Meadow - Tucker Prairie
    5: Cheney - Turnbull Wildlife Refuge (Loop 1)
    6: Cheney - Turnbull Wildlife Refuge (Loop 2)
    7: Spangle - Plaza
    8: Rockford - Hangman Valley
    9: Rockford - Waverly
  10: Fairfield - Tekoa Mountain - Waverly
Plus: The City and Outlying Areas of Spokane

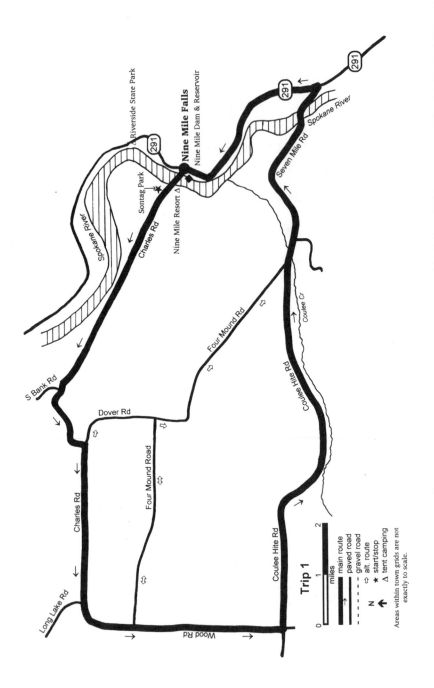

1. Sontag Park - Four Mound Prairie

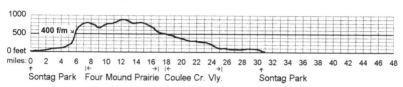

Miles: 21-31. After a steep, 2-mile climb, this close-in loop begins making its way through the open fields, pastures, and pine forests of Four Mound Prairie. (To skip the big hill, start at the 6.2-mile mark and at the 21.8-mile mark, turn left onto Four Mound Road to return to your car.) After turning onto Coulee Hite Road, the topography changes as the road wanders through a forested valley, following Coulee Creek down to the Spokane River. Traffic ranges from light to moderate, with the exception of a 3-mile stint on Highway 291, which becomes particularly busy, winding, and shoulderless in Nine Mile Falls.

Food/lodging/camping: *Nine Mile Falls*: Nine Mile Resort—showers (**509**-468-8422), Riverside State Park (456-3964). Two restaurants (276-8356, 467-1411).

Starting point: Nine Mile Falls is located approximately ten miles north of Spokane on Highway 291. After passing the dam, take the next left onto unmarked Charles Road. A half mile later, reach Sontag Park on the right-hand side of the road.

    0: From Sontag Park, **turn right** onto Charles Road. In less than a half mile, cross Hedin Road, which leads to Nine Mile Resort.

  4.4: South Bank Road intersects from the right as the shoulder widens and you begin a serious climb.

  6.2: **Turn right** at the T to stay on Charles Road (soon renamed Wood Road).

        Alt. route: To cut 10 miles off the trip, turn left onto Dover Road. Two miles later, bear left onto Four Mound Road and in another four miles, rejoin the main route at the 21.8-mile mark.

13.8: **Turn left** onto Coulee Hite Road, where traffic picks up a bit as you move through open farmland, wheat fields and of pine trees. The long, gradual descent along Coulee Creek begins.

21.8: Four Mound Road intersects from the left.

26.1: **Turn left** onto busy Highway 291.

29.7: Reach the *Nine Mile General Store* on the right. **Caution**: at this point the highway narrows and loses its shoulder as it winds through Nine Mile Falls. A reduction of the speed limit to 35 mph helps some.

30.1: Just past the dam, **turn left** onto Charles Road (unmarked) and return to Sontag Park on the right.

2. Deer Park - Williams Valley

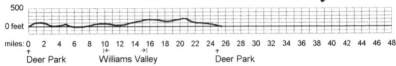

Miles: 25-48. Conveniently located just a few miles north of Spokane, this is the flattest ride in the region. Numerous side trips and alternate routes make it one of the most flexible, as well. Much of the trip is through the rural farmlands that lie at the base of the Selkirk Mountains in southeastern Stevens County. Traffic is light most of the way.

Food/lodging/camping: *Deer Park:* Pines RV Camp and Motel (509-276-2982), several restaurants and cafes. *Clayton:* tavern.

Starting point: Coming northbound on Highway 395, about 15 miles north of the Highway 395/Highway 2 junction, turn right at the McDonalds/Zips exit. This road becomes Main Avenue and takes you into Deer Park. Continue straight at the 4-way stop in town, crossing Crawford Street. Four blocks later, turn left on 4th Street, following the signs for Mix Park.

0: Head back to Main via 4th Street and cross Main Avenue.

0.6: **Turn right** onto N. Colville Street.

1.1: Pass the Jr. High school as you begin making your way into the countryside.

2.3: Cross Highway 395 and **turn left** onto Dalton Street.

4.5: **Turn right** onto Staley Road.

5.9: **Turn right** onto Monroe, where wheat fields become part of the scenery.

7.9: **Turn left** onto Burroughs Road.

10.9: *Side trip:* Turn left onto Swenson Road and follow it for nearly seven miles. Just before it drops steeply down to Highway 291, turn around and return to Burroughs Road.

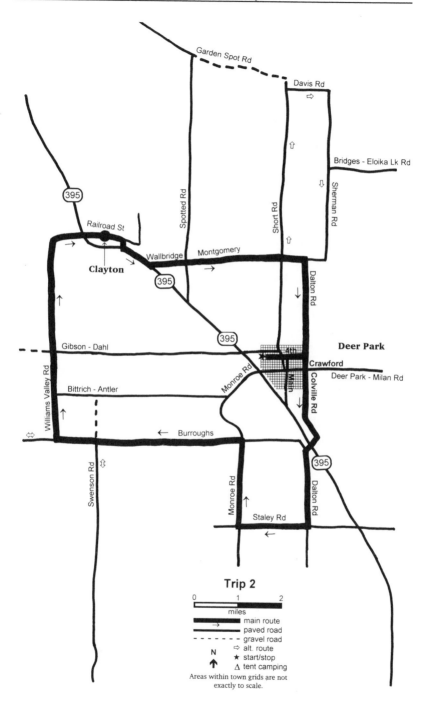

11.9: **Turn right** onto Williams Valley Road.

> *Side trip*: Continue straight to the end of the pavement (2.5 miles) and then return to this intersection. The road is flat and scenic all the way.

12.9: Bittrich-Antler Road intersects from the right.

> 13.9: *Alt. route*: To cut the trip short, turn right onto Gibson-Dahl Road and follow it five miles back to Deer Park, where it becomes 6th Street.

17.1: Cross Highway 395. There is a small grocery store at the junction.

17.4: **Turn right** onto Railroad Street.

17.8: Enter the mostly deserted town of Clayton. A tavern was open at the time of this survey.

18.1: **Bear right** where Furze Road intersects from the left.

18.3: **Turn left** onto Highway 395.

18.9: **Turn left** onto Wallbridge.

19.8: At the stop sign, continue straight as the road is renamed Montgomery.

> *Side trip*: Turn left onto Spotted Road, go five miles to Garden Spot Road, turn around and return to Montgomery.

> 21.7: *Side trip*: Turn left onto Short Road. After four miles, turn right onto Davis Road. A mile later, turn right onto Sherman Road. Four miles later, turn right onto Montgomery Road. A half mile later, rejoin the main route by turning left onto Dalton.

22.2: **Turn right** onto Dalton.

24.3: **Turn right** onto 4th Street, cross Main Avenue, and continue straight ahead to the city park.

3. Medical Lake - Silver Lake

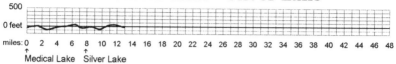

Miles: 13. Beginning at Waterfront Park in Medical Lake, the first half of this easy trip around Riddle Hill takes a mostly level course through open fields and woodlands. At the halfway point, the road passes right between Willow Lake and Granite Lake on its way to the east shore of Silver Lake. Traffic can be a bit bothersome on Medical Lake-Four Lakes Road, but the situation improves considerably once you reach Silver Lake Road.

Food/lodging/camping: *Medical Lake*: Ruby's RV Park & Campground (**509**-299-7829), Picnic Pines Campground (299-3223), Rainbow Cove Campground—showers (299-3717); restaurants, tavern, cafe, food stores.

Starting point: Medical Lake is located approximately 10 miles southeast of Spokane. From Highway 2, turn south onto Craig Road, follow it to Highway 902, and follow 902 west to Medical Lake. From I-90, take the Highway 902 exit. Find Waterfront Park along Highway 902 at the south end of town. Note: the park charges a $3.00 fee for parking on the weekends.

0: Return to the entrance of Waterfont Park and **turn left** onto the paved bike trail.

0.5: **Bear left** onto Jefferson, following the bike lane on the left side of the road.

1.0: **Turn right** on Lake Street, cross Lefevre Street, and continue straight.

2.1: Freeman Drive intersects from the right as the road you're on becomes Medical Lake-Four Lakes Road.

4.1: **Turn right** onto Medifor Road.

5.3: **Turn right** onto Medical Lake-Four Lakes Road.

5.5: **Turn right** onto Silver Lake Road.
    Side trip: Continue straight on Medical Lake-Four Lake Road to the town of Four Lakes.

6.5: The road swings to the right, and crosses right between Granite Lake and Willow Lake.

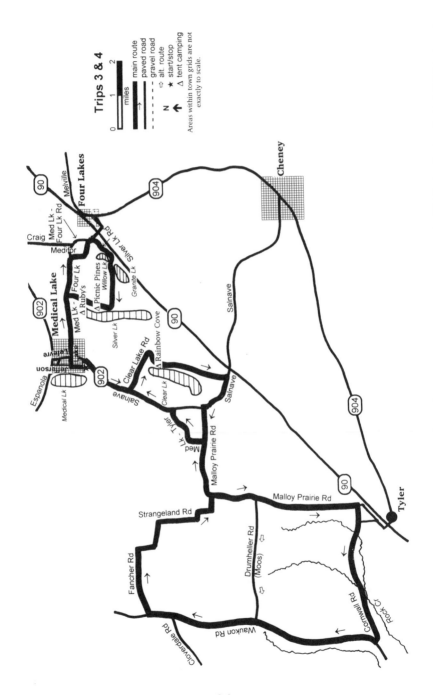

7.9: Reach the shores of Silver Lake.

8.9: Pass Picnic Pines Campground, a resort with a lounge.

9.4: **Turn left** onto Medical Lake-Four Lake Road.

11.3: Cross Lefevre Street. One Block later **turn left** onto Jefferson.

11.9: **Turn right** onto the paved bike path just before reaching Lefevre and follow it to Waterfront Park.

4. Med. Lk.- Bennett Meadow - Tucker Prairie

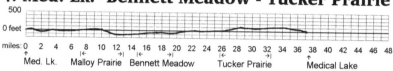

Miles: 30-37. This virtually flat loop has an unusually high reward-to-effort ratio. The first five miles of the route circle Clear Lake, moving through open fields, wetlands, woodlands and residential areas. At 8 miles, the scenery changes as you move through a 24-mile stretch of meadows, prairies, grazing land, and sagebrush. At 26 miles, you begin a 5-mile stretch on a remote back road that zig-zags its way through the rolling wheat fields of Tucker Prairie.

Food/lodging/camping/starting point: see trip 3.

0: Follow the one-way loop out of the parking lot.

0.1: **Turn left** onto Fancher-Connection Road.

0.3: **Turn right** onto Highway 902.

1.3: **Turn left** onto Clear Lake Road. Begin moving through open fields, wetlands, woodlands, and lake-shore residential areas.

2.5: Reach Rainbow Cove Resort.

5.3: **Turn right** onto Salnave Road.

6.7: **Turn left** onto Malloy Prairie Road and head into open wheat fields.

10.9: *Alt. route*: to shave 7 miles off the trip, turn right on Drumheller Road. Four miles later, turn right at the T, joining the main route at the 22.4-mile mark.

14.0: **Turn right** onto Cornwall Road and begin a 4-mile passage through Bennett Meadow.

18.4: **Turn right** onto Waukon Road (unmarked).

22.4: Drumheller Road (unmarked) intersects from the right.

25.7: **Turn right** onto Fancher Road (unmarked) just before crossing the RR tracks in the deserted town of Waukon. Move into an area of woodlands, open fields, marshes and meadows.

27.7: **Turn right** onto Strangeland Road (unmarked) and then stay with the pavement for the next 3.7 miles as it zigzags through Tucker Prairie.

31.4: **Turn left** onto Malloy Prairie Road.

33.0: **Turn left** onto Medical Lake-Tyler Road.

34.8: **Turn left** onto Salnave Road (Highway 902). Traffic picks up.

37.4: **Turn left** into Waterfront Park.

4a. Medical Lake (Lake Loop)

Most of this level, pleasant, 3-mile loop around Medical Lake is a paved bike (and pedestrian) trail. See trip 4 for details on getting to Waterfront Park.

0: Head north on the bike trail that begins at the park's entrance.

0.5: **Turn left** onto Jefferson—a bike lane is on the left side.

1.3: **Turn left** onto 4th Street and pass a small city park.

1.7: **Turn left** into the next small park. Follow the paved bike trail.

2.9: Reach the parking lot where you began.

5. Cheney - Turnbull Wildlife Refuge (Loop 1)

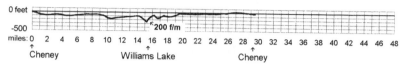

Miles: 29. With the exception of a one-mile, fairly steep climb up from Williams Lake, this scenic loop—open fields, woodlands, ponds, lakes, marshes, and resident wildlife—is virtually flat. The trip begins in Cheney, makes a 5-mile cruise through the Turnbull National Wildlife Refuge, drops to Williams Lake, where a resort makes a nice lunch stop, and then skirts the west boundary of the refuge on the way back to Cheney. Traffic is light except for a one-mile stint on Highway 904.

Food/lodging/camping: *Cheney:* Rosebrook Inn (**509**-235-6538), Willow Springs Motel (235-5138), Peaceful Pines RV & Campground—showers (235-4966), several restaurants. *Williams Lake:* Williams Lake Resort—camping, cabins, store, restaurant (235-2391).

Starting point: Cheney is located about 20 miles southeast of Spokane. From I-90, take the Four Lakes-Cheney exit (Highway 904). Pass through downtown Cheney and turn right onto Salnave Road. Six blocks later, turn left onto Eplin Street, and find parking at Salnave Park. Return to the intersection of Eplin and Salnave for the starting point.

0: **Turn right** onto Salnave Avenue.

0.3: **Turn left** onto W. 2nd Street at Moos Field.

0.5: **Turn right** onto K Street. Cross W. 1st Street (Highway 904) and the RR tracks. K Street becomes Cheney-Plaza Road.

4.9: Smith Road intersects from the left, which is the main entrance to Turnbull Wildlife Refuge and leads to headquarters, trail heads and wildlife viewing areas.

10.6: **Continue straight** onto Rock Lake Road, where Cheney-Plaza Road swings to the left.

12.1: **Turn right** onto Williams Lake Road, following the signs to Williams Lake Resort.

14.6: Badger Lake Road, which goes 1.5 miles to Badger Lake, intersects from the right.

15.5: Reach Williams Lake Resort—*store, restaurant, water, restrooms.*

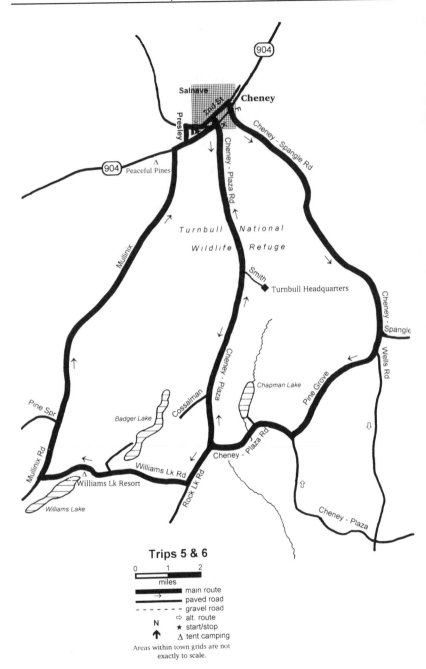

Trips 5 & 6

0   1   2
miles

main route
→ paved road
- - - - gravel road
⇨ alt. route
N ★ start/stop
↑ △ tent camping
Areas within town grids are not
exactly to scale.

16.5: Reach the crest of the hill as the scenery changes to wheat fields and sagebrush.

16.8: **Turn right** onto Mullinix Road.

18.6: Pine Springs Road, which goes two miles to Amber Lake, intersects from the left as you make your way into sparsely treed woodlands and open fields.

28.1: **Turn right** onto Highway 904, where there is an immediate increase in traffic.

28.8: **Turn left** onto Presley Drive.

29.1: **Turn right** onto Salnave Road.

29.3: **Turn right** onto Eplin.

6. Cheney - Turnbull Wildlife Refuge (Loop 2)

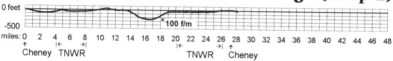

Miles: 27-34. The scenery, traffic conditions, length, and elevation profile of this trip are similar to Turnbull Loop #1, except the single hill is only half as steep. There is no meal stop on this trip. If you want to add extra miles to these easy loops, the trips are readily combined.

Food/lodging & starting point: see trip 5 for details.

0: **Turn right** onto Salnave from Eplin.

0.3: **Turn left** onto W. 2nd.

0.9: **Turn right** onto F Street, cross W. 1st Street (Highway 904). After crossing 6 sets of RR tracks, the road becomes Cheney-Spangle Road. Begin a level passage through open fields, woodlands, ponds, lakes, and marshes.

9.6: **Continue straight** onto Wells Road where Cheney-Spangle Road veers left. Traffic becomes very light.

10.0: **Turn right** onto Pine Grove Road and make your way through deserted wheat fields.

Alt. route: To expand the route by approximately 7 miles, continue straight onto Wells. Begin a series of roller-coaster hills as the road snakes its way through multi-colored, rolling wheat fields. About 6 miles later, turn right onto Cheney-Plaza Road. In another 5 miles, rejoin the main route at the 13.6-mile mark by continuing straight where Pine Grove Road intersects from the right.

13.6: **Turn right** onto Cheney-Plaza Road at the T.

15.0: Chapman Lake Road, which goes a half mile to Chapman Lake, intersects from the right.

16.6: **Bear right** to stay on Cheney-Plaza Road. The scenery returns to a mixture of woodlands, fields, marshes, ponds, wetlands.

22.3: Smith Road, the main entrance to Turnbull National Wildlife Refuge, intersects from the right. This road accesses trail heads and wildlife viewing areas.

26.6: Cross the Highway (W. 1st Street).

26.7: **Turn left** onto W. 2nd Street.

26.9: **Turn right** onto Salnave Avenue.

27.3: **Turn left** onto Eplin.

7. Spangle - Plaza

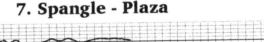

Miles: 18-28. This medium-length loop wanders through the rolling wheat fields without challenging the cyclist with any significant hills. Panoramic views of the mountains to the northeast on the last third of the trip add some variety to this peaceful, nearly level romp through the fields on lightly traveled back roads.

Food/lodging/camping: *Spangle*: restaurant (**509**-245-3552), mini-mart & gas station, tavern (245-3227). No lodging. No services en route.

Starting point: Approximately 15 miles south of Spokane, from Highway 195, turn east onto Cheney-Spangle Road. Turn left onto Main and then right onto E. 3rd Street and proceed to the small city park.

0: From the park, return to the intersection of E. 3rd Street and Main. **Turn left** onto Main. Proceed through town. Main becomes Old Highway 195.

1.2: Spangle-Waverly Road intersects from the left as the route passes through rolling fields of wheat and peas.

6.2: *Alt. route:* To cut approximately 10 miles from the route, turn right onto Powers Road. After about 4.5 miles, bear right onto Sherman. Follow Sherman for another 3.5 miles,

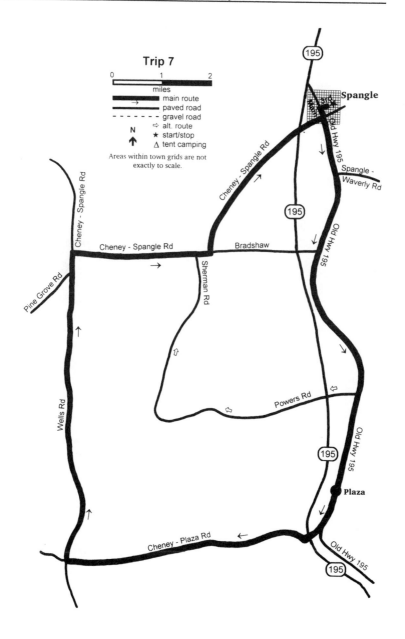

turning right onto Cheney-Spangle Road to rejoin the main route at the 23.5-mile mark.

8.2: Enter the town of Plaza—no services or stores.

9.1: **Turn right** onto Cheney-Plaza Road; pass under Highway 195.

14.4: **Turn right** onto Wells Road.

19.4: Reach panoramic views of forested hills behind wheat and alfalfa fields.

21.0: **Turn right** onto Cheney-Spangle Road. Traffic picks up a bit here as you begin a series of shallow roller-coaster hills.

23.5: Sherman Road intersects from the right.

23.7: **Turn left** to stay on Cheney-Spangle as the road ahead of you becomes Bradshaw.

26.8: Cross Highway 195.

27.5: **Turn left** onto Main Street.

27.6: **Turn right** onto E. 3rd Street and return to the park.

8. Rockford - Hangman Valley

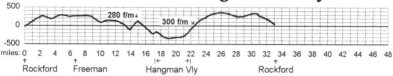

Miles: 33. This loop begins in rolling wheat fields bordered by mountains before winding through the meadows, creeks, and cliffs of scenic Hangman Valley. After climbing steeply out of the valley, it's back to the open fields for the last third of the trip. Traffic volumes—moderate on Highway 27 and the Palouse Highway—decrease significantly after reaching Valley Chapel Road at the 15-mile mark. Use extra caution on the last 2.5 miles of the Palouse Highway, where there is little or no shoulder.

Food/lodging/camping: *Rockford*: no lodging, one restaurant (509-291-4313). There is a small grocery store in Freeman.

Starting point: Just east of Spokane on I-90, take Highway 27 southbound. Approximately 17 miles later, turn left onto Highway 278, following signs for Rockford. Six blocks later, turn right at the flashing light (First Street), staying with Highway 278. One block later, find the city park on the right.

    0: From the park, **turn left** onto Highway 278.

0.05: **Turn left** at the three-way stop, staying with Highway 278.

  0.5: **Turn right** onto Highway 27, where there is a generous shoulder and traffic is moderate. To the east, behind rolling wheat fields, are the forested hills that run along the Idaho border.

  4.7: Elder Road intersects from the right.

  6.7: Enter the community of Freeman, which has a small *grocery store*.

  8.3: **Turn left** onto the Palouse Highway. Traffic remains moderate.

  8.6: Darknell Road intersects from the left.

10.2: Old Palouse Highway intersects from the right.

12.7: *Caution*: For the next 2.5 miles there is little or no shoulder.

15.2: **Turn left** onto Valley Chapel Road, where there is a significant decrease in traffic as you make your way into the woodlands.

19.1: Reach the confluence of Hangman Creek and California

33

Creek—a fine place to take a break. The road ahead is beautiful and peaceful, winding its way through wooded areas, meadows, and wheat fields. Swallows nest by the hundreds in the tall cliffs that border the far side of the creek.

21.7: The climb out of the valley begins rather steeply and moderates 1.5 miles later. In another 2 miles, you get a sweeping view of multi-colored wheat fields.

27.1: **Bear left** to stay on Valley-Chapel Road where N. Kentuck Trails Road intersects from the right. Begin a series of moderate roller coasters.

30.0: **Bear left** to stay on Valley-Chapel Road where Jackson intersects from the right. Watch for a ***rough RR crossing*** a mile later.

32.4: **Turn left** onto Highway 27.

32.5: **Turn right** onto Highway 278, following signs to Rockford.

33.1: **Turn right** at the flashing light, following signs for Highway 278, and return to the park.

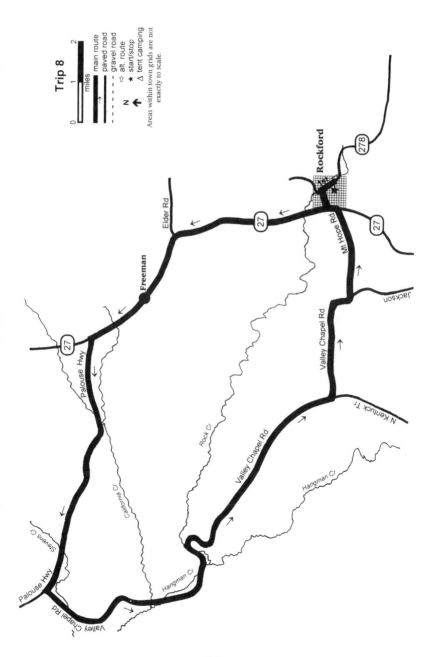

Trip 8

miles
0 1 2

main route
paved route
gravel road
alt. route
☆ start/stop
★ start/stop
△ tent camping

N ←

Areas within town grids are not
exactly to scale.

Rockford

278

Elder Rd

27

Mt Hope Rd

27

Freeman

Jackson

Palouse Hwy

27

Valley Chapel Rd

Rock Cr

N Kentuck Tr

California Cr

Valley Chapel Rd

Hangman Cr

Stevens Cr

Palouse Hwy

Valley Chapel Rd

Hangman Cr

9. Rockford - Waverly

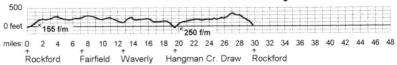

Miles: 30. After making a moderate, 2-mile climb at the beginning of this cruise through rolling wheat fields, you are rewarded with a magnificent view of the mountains to the north and east. There are no serious hills, although there are far more short, shallow ups and downs than the elevation profile admits. Traffic is very light all the way except for two quick stints on Highway 27. Fairfield and Waverly offer cafes and parks for R&R.

Food/lodging: *Rockford*: no lodging, cafe (**509**-291-4313). *Fairfield*: cafe (283-2489), grocery store. *Waverly*: bar & grill (283-2398).

Starting point: see trip 8.

0: **Turn left** onto Highway 278 (the street you came in on).

0.05: **Turn left** at the three-way stop, staying with Highway 278.

0.5: **Turn left** onto Highway 27. Traffic is fairly light.

0.7: **Turn right** onto Mt. Hope Road, and begin a moderately steep climb. Traffic is very light.

2.3: Reach a marvelous view of wheat fields and mountains.

3.0: **Turn left** onto Jackson at the T.

4.8: Palouse Road intersects from the left.

6.1: **Turn right** onto Highway 27, where traffic picks up a little.

7.4: In Fairfield, **turn right** onto W. Carlton Avenue (becomes Prairie View Road), following the sign to Waverly. Traffic is extremely light.
Side trip: Continue straight into Fairfield—*water* and *restrooms* at the park, a *cafe*, and a *grocery store*.

12.0: **Bear right** onto Spangle-Waverly Road.
Side trip: Turn left and ride .5 miles to Waverly—*tavern* with food; *water* and *restrooms* at the park.

16.8: **Turn right** onto N. Kentuck Trail Road.

18.9: W. Bradshaw Road intersects from the right as you begin a descent to Hangman Creek.

24.0: **Turn right** onto Valley Chapel Road after passing a cemetery.

26.8: **Bear left** to stay on Valley Chapel/Mt. Hope Road where Jackson Road intersects from the right.

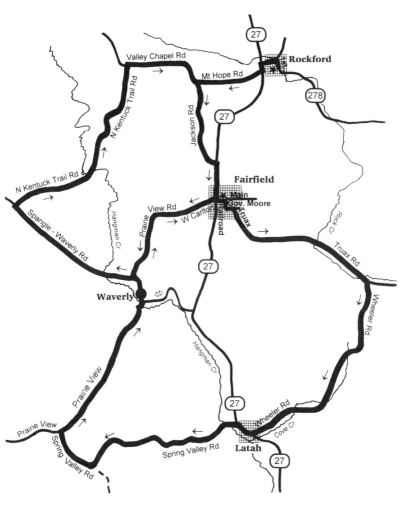

Trips 9 & 10

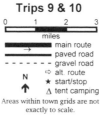

miles

main route
→ paved road
- - - - - gravel road
⇨ alt. route
N ★ start/stop
↑ △ tent camping

Areas within town grids are not
exactly to scale.

28.1: **Caution:** rough RR crossing.

29.1: **Turn left** onto Highway 27.

29.3: **Turn right** onto Highway 278, following signs for Rockford.

29.8: **Turn right** at the flashing light, staying with Highway 278 and return to the city park.

10. Fairfield - Tekoa Mountain - Waverly

Miles: 33. This scenic loop heads straight for Tekoa Mountain after leaving Fairfield. On Truax Road—the first 6 miles of the trip—you'll enjoy panoramic views of open wheat fields and the surrounding forested hills. Two miles after turning south on Wheeler Road, you'll find yourself smack dab at the base of Tekoa Mountain, moving through a blend of woodlands and fields. After leaving Latah, the scenery changes dramatically as you wind ten miles through hilly wheat fields on narrow, seldom-traveled Spring Valley Road. In Waverly, a side trip offers a scenic, 6-mile, out-and-back trip along Hangman Creek. Traffic ranges from very light to nearly nonexistent.

Food/lodging/camping: *Fairfield*: no lodging, cafe (**509**-283-2489). *Latah*: cafe (286-4444). *Waverly*: bar & grill (283-2398).

Starting point: Just east of Spokane on I-90, take Highway 27 southbound. Approximately 23 miles later, you'll be in Fairfield. Turn left onto Main and find parking at the city park.

0: Head into town (eastbound) on Main. After crossing the RR tracks, **turn right** onto Railroad Avenue.

0.1: **Bear left** onto E. Gov. Moore Street.

0.3: **Bear right** as the road becomes Truax. Traffic is very light as you begin a moderate, 2-mile climb. At the crest, you get a panoramic view of wheat fields and mountains.

6.3: **Turn right** onto Wheeler Road.

8.4: Painter Road intersects from the left.

8.7: You're at the base of Tekoa Mountain as you begin a long descent into Latah.

13.4: Enter the community of Latah—*cafe*, no other services.

13.7: Cross Melvin-100 Street and continue straight on what is now northbound Highway 27.

14.0: **Turn left** just outside of town onto Spring Valley Road. Cross Hangman Creek and begin a 7-mile stretch along this narrow, lightly traveled road that winds back and forth, up and down through multi-colored wheat fields.

14.2: Cross Hangman Creek.

21.8: **Turn right** onto Prairie View Road.

22.8: Ray Road intersects from the right.

27.1: **Bear left** just after crossing over Hangman Creek (unmarked), staying with Prairie View Road where Waverly road intersects from the right.

> *Side trip*: For a trip through peaceful Hangman Creek Valley, take Waverly Road all the way to Highway 27 and back.

27.4: Reach the city park—*restrooms, shade, water*. There is also a *tavern* in town that serves food.

28.0: **Bear right** to stay on Prairie View Road as Spangle-Waverly Road intersects from the left. Begin the gradual, 200-foot climb out of Waverly.

32.5: **Turn right** onto 1st Street and go one block to the park.

The City and Outlying Areas of Spokane

Spokane is Washington's second largest city. Several major highways converge upon the area, and traffic can be fairly intense at times. The purpose of this section—and the accompanying maps—is two-fold. One, to help cyclists select routes in, out, and through the city; and two, to help Spokane cyclists find their way out of the city and onto the back roads that lie only a few miles beyond the city limits. Due to space limitations, many cross streets are not included on the maps. If you are not at least somewhat familiar with Spokane, highlighting these routes on a full-size city map (available free from Spokane Information Center—see Appendix) will help keep you on course.

Passing Through

Bikes are prohibited on Interstate 90 and on Division Street (Highway 395) from downtown Spokane to the junction with the Newport Highway (Highway 2).

Without a doubt, the best east-west route is the Centennial Trail. The trail is paved the entire way, passes through a number of state and regional parks, and is off limits to motorized vehicles. Maximum speed is 15 mph. There are a number of access points—many of which are indicated on the accompanying map. Contact the *Friends of the Centennial Trail* (see Appendix) for a detailed map of the entire route and for information to enhance your enjoyment of the trail.

Picking a north-south route is a little more difficult. North of the Spokane River, a direct route commonly used by area cyclists is the Post-Wall-Mill route on the west side of Division (Highway 395). South of the river, Post and Wall are busy, one-way streets. In this section of town, Howard will get you north and south between Boone and 2nd Street. Cyclists may use the paved path through Riverfront Park, which is part of the Centennial Trail route, to cross the river (maximum speed is 6 mph). On the east side, Addison-Standard-Colton and Freya-Market are the two primary north-south routes. Aside from these direct routes, consult the Spokane Area map for other bikable streets—most of these are either routes recommended by the Spokane Regional Transportation Council or routes commonly used by cyclists.

Rides in the outlying areas

Although most of the roads that pass through the outlying areas of Spokane have traffic levels too high for that genuine, transcendental back-roads feeling, below are some areas through which you will find some enjoyable cycling. Use the maps to design your own customized loops over the roads listed after each area. In addition to cycling in these areas, a seasoned cyclist can ride from Spokane, do trips 1, 2, 3, 4, 5, 6, or 8, and return to Spokane in the same day. The details on the routes out of town will assist you in getting to these trips.

Five Mile Prairie: Five Mile Road, Woodside, Indian Trail, and Rutter Parkway are the basic ingredients to this hilly route.

Deer Park: This area extends further north than the area covered on maps in this chapter. Consult the trip-connector map and the map for trip 2 for more details.

Monroe will get you from the north end of Spokane up to trip 2. From there, you can do all or part of trip 2 or continue on Monroe until it crosses Highway 395 and goes into Deer Park, where it becomes Crawford. Continue on Crawford all the way through Deer Park, where the road is renamed Deer Park-Milan. Follow Deer-Park Milan across Highway 2 and over to Milan Road. Head south on Milan to its junction with Highway 2. Turn left onto Highway 2 and, a half mile later, turn right on Dennison-Chattaroy Road. Follow Dennison-Chattaroy across Highway 395 and back to Monroe. Turn left on Monroe and follow Monroe back to the north end of Spokane.

Valley Prairie: Basic building blocks include the following roads: Big Meadows, Day Mt. Spokane, Green Bluff, Yale.

Peone Prairie: Day Mt. Spokane, Madison, Forker, Moffat, Peone, Market, Yale. *Caution*: From Highway 206 to Bigelow Gulch, Forker is narrow and tends to attract over-the-speed-limit motorists. South of Bigelow Gulch, Forker is definitely not for cyclists. Use Lehman to get to Millwood if you wish to extend your trip further south.

Pleasant Prairie: Peone, Moffat, Forker, Pleasant Prairie (or Bigelow Gulch), Bruce, Stoneman, Market.

Newman Lake: Starr to E. Newman Lake Road and W. Newman Lake Road.

Centennial Trail: The 37-mile, paved trail runs from Nine Mile Falls to the Idaho border, where it becomes the Idaho Centennial Trail and continues several more paved miles to Post Falls and Coeur d'Alene. Except for a section running through downtown Spokane and along Upper River Drive, the trail is off limits to motorized vehicles.

Medical Lake: see the route to Lincoln County below.

41

Indian Prairie/Medical Lake: Take the Centennial Trail or Aubrey White Parkway to Seven Mile Road (the southern border of trip 1). Follow Seven Mile Road to Wood Road. Turn left onto Wood, follow it across Highway 2 onto Espanola Road. Follow Espanola Road into Medical Lake. From Medical Lake, take Medical Lake-Four Lakes Road (see trip 3) into Four Lakes. From Four Lakes, take Melville Road to Spotted Road. Turn left onto Spotted, right onto Hallet, and left onto Grove. Grove will take you across I-90 to Geiger. Turn left onto Geiger, right onto Electric, and right onto Hayford. After crossing Highway 2, follow the bike route onto what eventually becomes Trails Road, which joins Government Way after crossing the Centennial Trail. From Government Way, turn left onto Fort Wright Drive to Cross the Spokane River and return to the heart of Spokane.

Colbert to Elk: From Colbert, combine Elk-Chattaroy Road, Milan Road, and a short stretch of Highway 2 for a loop to the town of Elk. See the trip-connector map for coverage of the northern portion of this loop.

Getting to the Back Road Loops

To choose a route out of the city and into the back country, use the maps in this chapter to get yourself from your starting location to the outbound routes described below. For extended trips use the trip-connector maps to get from one loop to the next.

Stevens County: Follow the instructions above for getting to Deer Park and trip 2.

Pend Oreille County: Find your way to Mead and then take Market, Yale, Elk-Chattaroy (or Milan), and Camden to trip 22. LeClerc Road out of Newport will get you to trip 30, and keep you smiling all the way. *Caution*: Camden Road is very narrow and steep.

Southern Spokane & Whitman counties: There are several options, depending on where you're starting from. One: Take Dishman-Mica Road to its junction with Highway 27. Then, take Highway 27 to trip 8 and points south. Two: Take the Palouse Highway south to trip 8 and points south. Three: Take Inland Empire to 23rd, turn right on 23rd, bear left at the top of the hill, and cross Highway 195 onto Thorpe. About 3 miles later, turn left onto Grove, right onto Hallet, and then left on Spotted Road. Two miles later, turn right onto Andrus and follow it to Cheney-Spokane. Turn right onto Cheney-Spokane and follow it into Cheney—the starting point of trips 5 and 6.

Lincoln County: Take Inland Empire to 23rd, turn right onto 23rd, bear left at the top of the hill, and cross 195 onto Thorpe. About 3 miles later, turn left onto Grove, and then right onto Hallet. Follow

Hallet across I-90 and onto Highway 902. Highway 902 will take you into Medical Lake. From here, consult the trip-connector map to select a route to your Lincoln County destination.

Northeastern Spokane County: Take the Centennial Trail or Aubrey White Parkway to Seven Mile Road (trip 1).

Spokane Area Map #1

0   1   2
miles

N ↑

— primary hwy
— bikable street
- - - gravel road
••• Centennial Tr.
◆ C. Tr. access
▨ park/lake

© 1998 Silcox Productions
Duplication by any means is
illegal.

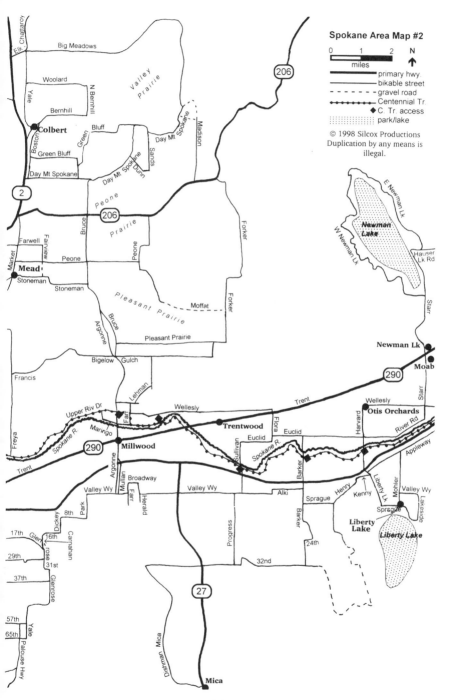

Only 15 miles west of Spokane, Four Mound Prairie offers an escape from heavy traffic (trip 1).

Devil's Canyon, just above the Snake River (trip 21)

5

Lincoln, Adams, & Franklin Counties

The sparsely populated counties of Lincoln, Adams and Franklin offer some of the most traffic-free cycling in the state. You'll find a physical and mental space that defies description as you ride through rock-walled basins, ice-age flood channels, rolling wheat fields, sagebrush, coulees, mesas, canyons, and river valleys.

Several of the longer loops are quite flat, offering good training opportunities for cyclists working on building up their saddle tolerance.

Many of these back roads are not marked. However, all intersecting paved roads are shown on the map, making it easy to keep track of junctions and stay on course.

For the most part, this is an exposed, arid area, making it ideal for early- and late-season trips. When cycling these areas in the summer months, be prepared for potentially intense heat and sunshine. Study the route descriptions carefully and pack plenty of water and food for long stretches without water, restaurants, stores, or other services.

Trips:

11: Reardan - Spring Creek Canyon - Devil's Gap
12: Reardan - Waukon - Edwall
13: Davenport - Bluestem
14: Harrington - Channeled Scablands - Odessa
15: Harrington - Lord's Valley
16: Sprague - Crab Creek Scablands
17: Sprague - Williams Lake - Ewan
18: Wilbur - Wilson Creek Flood Channel
19: Wilbur North
20: Washtucna - Palouse River - Staley Coulee
21: Connell - Snake River - Devil's Canyon

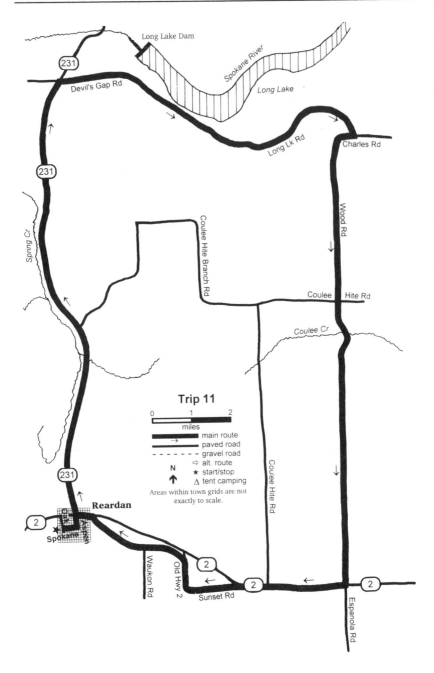

Trip 11

```
0        1        2
    miles
━━━━━━━  main route
─────── paved road
- - - - - gravel road
⇨ alt. route
N        ★ start/stop
↑        △ tent camping
Areas within town grids are not
        exactly to scale.
```

11. Reardan - Spring Cr. Canyon - Devil's Gap

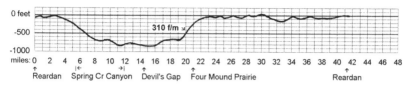

Miles: 41. After leaving Reardan, the first half of this ever-changing route makes a seven-mile descent into scenic Spring Creek Canyon, passes through Devil's Gap, rambles along the southern ridge of the Spokane River, and then climbs up to Four Mound Prairie. The second half begins with an 8-mile, level cruise through the prairie. After a short, steep descent to Coulee Creek comes a series of shallow roller-coaster hills in the wheat fields of Indian Prairie, followed by a 5-mile stretch of an all-but-abandoned section of old Highway 2.

Food/lodging/camping: Reardan has a small grocery store and drive-in, but no motels. See trip 13 for details on lodging in Davenport.

Starting point: Reardan is located approximately 25 miles west of Spokane on Highway 2. To get to the Reardan city park, turn south on Oak Street (at the library) and go two blocks.

  0: From the park, head north on Oak, then **turn right** onto Spokane.

0.2: **Turn left** onto Aspen. Two blocks later, cross Highway 2 as Aspen becomes Highway 231, taking you through open wheat fields. Traffic varies seasonally, but is usually quite tolerable.

4.2: The shoulder narrows as you continue a steady, gradual descent into forested Spring Creek Canyon.

4.8: **Bear left** at the Y to stay on Highway 231.

12.0: **Turn right** onto Devil's Gap Road, which later becomes Long Lake Road. Here, you'll find a significant decrease in traffic. Ospreys circle overhead as you move through pine woodlands and wildlife viewing areas.

19.6: Gray Road intersects from the left as you begin a fairly steep climb to Four Mound Prairie.

21.0: **Turn right** onto Charles Road (soon renamed Wood Road). Traffic is extremely light, and the climb is nearly done.

25.4: Coulee Hite Road intersects right and left.

26.0: Descend steeply to the Coulee Creek draw—a little oasis amid the arid wheat fields. Soon you'll begin a series of more than 20 shallow roller-coaster hills on your way through Indian Prairie.

32.8: **Turn right** onto Highway 2. Traffic is moderate to heavy, but the shoulder is smooth and wide.

35.5: **Bear left** onto unmarked Old Highway 2 (Sunset Road)—a cracked-concrete, somewhat rough road.

> *Alt. route:* To avoid the rough roadway and a quarter-mile stretch of gravel, stay with Highway 2 all the way back to Reardan. The tradeoff is more traffic. You'll also miss out on a very intimate encounter with acres of *amber waves of grain.*

37.0: **Bear left** onto a quarter-mile stretch of gravel road and then rejoin the now-improved concrete road.

40.4: **Turn left** onto Highway 2.

40.6: **Turn left** onto Aspen.

40.7: **Turn right** onto Spokane.

41.2: **Turn left** onto Oak and return to the park.

12. Reardan - Waukon - Edwall

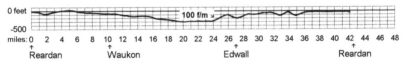

Miles: 29-42. This mostly flat trip through multi-colored wheat fields, sagebrush, wildflowers, marshes and wetlands is perfect for cyclists seeking an early-season trip, an introduction to longer rides, or genuine solitude. The biggest challenges are the lack of shade on much of the route and a moderate, 2-mile climb at the 25-mile mark. Just beyond the half-way point, the quaint town of Edwall, with a small cafe and well-manicured city park, makes a nice lunch stop. Except for a couple of brief encounters with Highway 2, traffic is extremely light the entire way.

Food/lodging/camping & starting point: *Reardan*: see trip 11 for details. *Edwall*: Sully's Cafe (509-236-2280).

0: From the park, head north on Oak Street and then turn right onto Spokane.

0.4: **Turn left** onto Aspen Street.

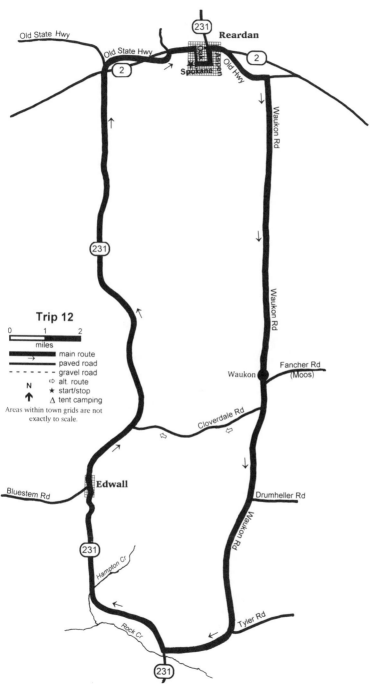

Old State Hwy

Old State Hwy

231 **Reardan**

2

2

Old Hwy

Spokane

Waukon Rd

Waukon Rd

231

Trip 12

0   1   2
miles

━━━ main route
→   paved road
- - - gravel road
⇨   alt. route
★   start/stop
△   tent camping

N

Areas within town grids are not
exactly to scale.

Fancher Rd
(Moos)

Waukon

Cloverdale Rd

Bluestem Rd

Edwall

Drumheller Rd

Waukon Rd

231

Hampton Cr

Rock Cr

Tyler Rd

231

0.45: **Turn right** onto Highway 2.

0.7: **Turn right** onto the old concrete-slab highway (unmarked).

> *Alt. route*: Continue straight on Highway 2. About 1.5 miles later, turn right onto Waukon Road and rejoin the main route at the 2.3-mile mark.

2.3: **Turn right** onto Waukon Road (unmarked), where the asphalt feels especially nice after the bumpety-bump of concrete slabs.

10.6: Reach the deserted town of Waukon.

> 11.3: *Alt. route*: To cut 13 miles off the trip, turn right onto Cloverdale Road (unmarked). Four miles later, at the junction with Highway 231, turn right, joining the main route at the 28.6-mile mark.

20.2: At the T, **turn right** onto Highway 231 and head toward Edwall.

27.0: Reach Edwall. **Turn right** at the fire station.

> *Side trip*: Just before this point, near the post office, a paved road intersecting from the left will take you to Sully's Cafe.

27.2: Reach the town park, where you'll find water, grass, trees, and shade—welcome commodities in these parts.

28.6: Cloverdale Road (unmarked) intersects from the right.

39.3: Cross Highway 2. A half mile later, turn right onto the old, concrete highway.

> *Alt. route*: Turn right onto Highway 2 and follow it 3 miles back to Reardan.

40.7: Cross Highway 2 again.

41.6: **Turn right** onto Highway 2.

42.5: **Turn right** onto Oak Street and go one block to the city park.

12a. Edwall Loop

For a 21-mile, relatively easy loop, begin at the Edwall city park and head north on Highway 231. The 5-mile stretch of Cloverdale Road is quite level. See trip 12 (from mile mark 11.3 to mile mark 27.2) for details on the rest of the route.

1.4: **Turn right** onto Cloverdale Road (unmarked).

5.4: At the T, **turn right** onto Waukon Road.

14.3: **Turn right** onto Highway 231.

21.1 **Turn right** at the fire station in Edwall, and return to the park.

13. Davenport - Bluestem

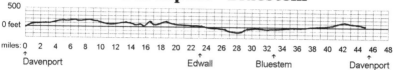

Miles: 45. While there is a bit more climbing on this route than the elevation profile indicates (due to a number of roller-coaster hills too small to appear on the graph), this loop has no significant hills. The first half of the trip is comprised mostly of wheat fields and sagebrush. At the midway point, in Edwall, the city park and Sully's Cafe provide options for a lunch stop. A few miles beyond Edwall, thanks to Bluestem Creek, the scenery changes to tree farms, ponds, wetlands, groves of conifers, and views into the lush creek basin. Then it's back to wheat fields and sagebrush for the rest of the trip. Traffic is very light except for an 8-mile stretch of Highway 28.

Food/lodging/camping: *Davenport:* Black Bear Motel (**509**-725-7700), Davenport Motel—non-smoking only (725-7071), several restaurants. *Edwall:* Sully's Cafe (236-2280).

Starting point: Davenport is located 36 miles west of Spokane on Highway 2. To get to the city park, turn south on 6th and go one block.

  0: Head north on 6th and cross Highway 2.
   Alt. route: To avoid 4 miles of bumpy, cracked pavement on the first part of Old Highway 2, turn right on Highway 2, and rejoin the main route at the 11.2-mile mark.
0.1: **Turn right** onto Sinclair Street.
0.5: Cross Highway 25 and continue east on Old Highway 2 (unmarked).
3.4: **Bear right** and cross the RR tracks.
10.9: **Bear right** and head for the junction of Highway 2 and Highway 231.
11.2: Cross Highway 2 and head south on Highway 231, where traffic is light and there is an adequate shoulder.
15.0: To the right, Crab Creek makes its way through Pleasant Valley.
21.7: Cloverdale Road (unmarked) intersects from the left.
23.2: Reach Edwall. The city park is on the right, offering *water*, a green lawn, and shade.

23.6: **Turn right** onto Bluestem Road (unmarked). A *cafe* is at the junction—no other stores or services in town. Soon you'll get a change of scenery—trees, ponds, wetlands, wildlife, and views of the creek basin—as you enter an area irrigated by Bluestem Creek.

32.9: Enter Bluestem—a couple of houses, grain-storage silos, and a grange hall.

36.8: **Turn right** onto Highway 28, which has very smooth pavement and wide shoulders in addition to a significant increase in traffic. This stretch of moderately busy highway makes one appreciate anew what the back roads have to offer.

43.4: **Turn right** onto Tyler Road (unmarked).

44.1: **Turn left** onto Third Street.

44.7: **Turn left** onto Main Street.

44.9: **Turn right** onto 6th Street and return to the city park.

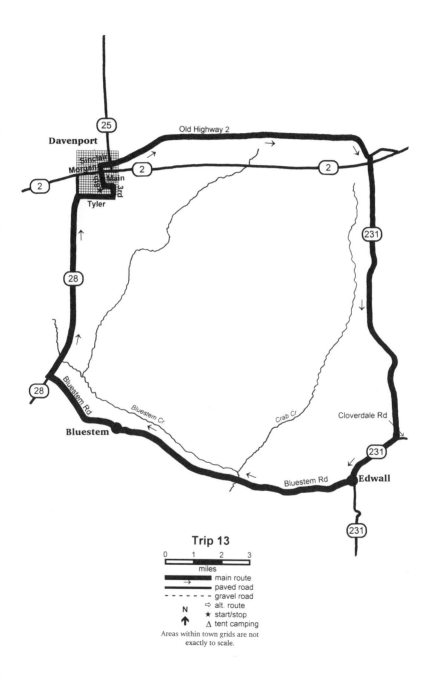

Old Highway 2

Davenport

Sinclair
Morgan
Main
Tyler

Bluestem Rd

Bluestem Cr

Crab Cr

Cloverdale Rd

Bluestem

Bluestem Rd

Edwall

Trip 13

0   1   2   3
miles

main route
→ paved road
- - - - gravel road
⇨ alt. route
N ★ start/stop
↑ △ tent camping

Areas within town grids are not
exactly to scale.

55

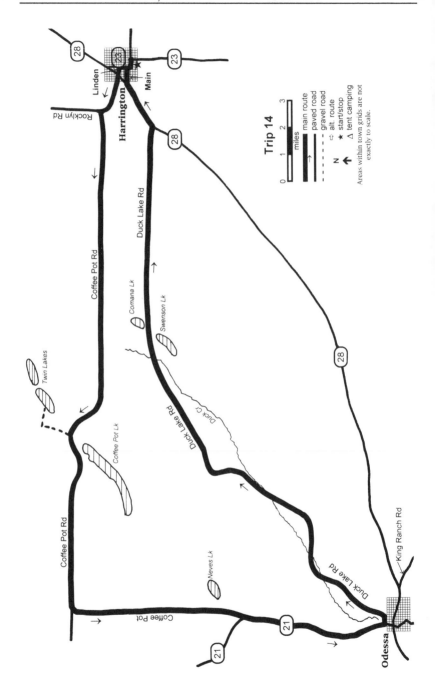

14. Harrington - Scablands - Odessa

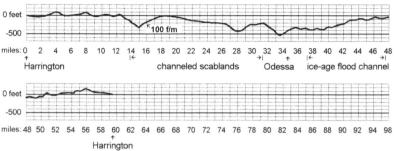

Miles: 60. Over many ups and downs too subtle to show on the elevation profile, this route passes through open wheat fields, sagebrush, and channeled scablands—enormous rocky basins containing creeks, lakes, wetlands, and ponds carved out of the earth more than 12,000 years ago by glacial flooding. At the 15-mile mark, a short side trip on a gravel road takes you to Twin Lakes Canyon, where there are endless roads and trails to explore. At the midway point, another short side trip leads to the charming town of Odessa—a nice lunch stop. Except for short stints on Highway 21 and Highway 28, you'll have the road to yourself much of the time.

Food/lodging/camping: *Harrington*: no lodging, 2 cafes. *Odessa*: Odessa Motel (**509**-982-2412), 2 restaurants (982-2377, 982-0111).

Starting point: From Davenport (36 miles east of Spokane), head south on Highway 28. Fourteen miles later, follow the signs for Highway 23 into Harrington. On the far side of town, after bearing left to stay on Highway 23, find the city park just across the tracks.

  0: From the park, **turn left** onto Highway 23 and follow it back through town.

0.4: After crossing Alice Road, go one block and **turn left** onto Linden (unmarked). Cross Highway 28, and continue straight onto Coffee Pot Road (unmarked). Begin making your way up and down a series of roller-coaster hills and through a mixture of sagebrush and wheat fields.

2.3: **Bear left** at the Y, staying with Coffee Pot Road, as Rocklyn Road (unmarked) intersects from the right.

14.6: *Side trip*: For a trip into scenic Twin Lakes Canyon, turn right on the gravel public-land access road. At 1.5 miles,

57

reach the gravel road leading to Twin Lakes—another two miles down the road. The many trails in the area offer hours of exploration.

21.3: At the Y, **bear left** to stay with unmarked Coffee Pot Road. Begin another series of moderate roller-coasters through the wheat fields.

27.9: Reach the bottom of a 200-foot descent to Crab Creek, which flows through a green, irrigated valley.

27.7: **Turn left** onto Highway 21 (unmarked), where traffic picks up a bit and the shoulder is marginal. After a moderate, 3-mile climb, you begin the descent into Odessa.

33.7: **Turn left** onto Duck Lake Road (unmarked) at a power substation, and begin another long series of roller-coaster hills through this ice-age flood channel.
Side trip: Continue straight for a quarter mile to the town of Odessa—*cafes, park*.

56.8: **Turn left** onto Highway 28 (unmarked). Although traffic picks up here, there is a three-foot shoulder.

59.2: **Turn right** onto Main, which is the first paved road leading into Harrington.

59.4: **Turn right** onto Third Street (Highway 23).

59.5: **Bear left**, staying with Highway 23, cross the tracks, and return to the park.

15. Harrington - Lord's Valley

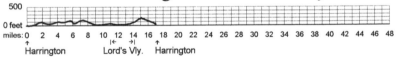

Miles: 17. While there are numerous shallow roller-coaster hills on this short loop, there are no significant hills. Scenery is primarily rolling wheat fields, with the grazing lands of flat, irrigated Lord's Valley providing a pleasant change of pace. Traffic is light on Tokio Road and Mohler Road, and ranges from light to moderate on Highway 23, which has an adequate shoulder. No services en route.

Food/lodging/camping & starting point: see trip 14.

0: From the park, **turn right** onto Highway 23. One block later, **turn right** onto Tokio Road (unmarked).

0.2: Landmark: pass a cemetery on the left.

5.1: **Turn left** onto Mohler Road (unmarked).

7.6: At the top of the hill, you get a panoramic view of wheat fields.

8.9: At the T, **turn left** onto Highway 23.

12.1: Enter Lord's Valley, irrigated by Lord's Creek and several smaller streams.

13.3: Armstrong road intersects from the right as you begin the climb out of the valley.

17.1: Enter Harrington and return to the park (on the left).

16. Sprague - Crab Creek Scablands

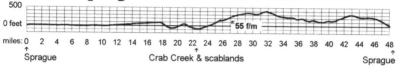

Miles: 48-61. Beginning in Sprague, this loop moves along the shore of Sprague Lake before rising gently into the wheat fields. At the midway point, Tokio Road makes a two-stage, 200-foot drop to Crab Creek, which flows through a scabland flood channel on DNR land. Here, there are numerous opportunities for off-road explorations. After climbing out of the scablands (a very gradual, nine-mile ascent), you begin a series of shallow hills, making your way through rolling wheat fields. Along Highway 23, Lord's Creek and Sheep Creek make their way to Crab Creek, creating ponds and wetlands—nesting habitat for myriad varieties of birds. Until you reach Highway 23, where volume picks up a bit, traffic is extremely light.

Food/lodging/camping: *Sprague*: Purple Sage Motel (**509**-257-2507), Last Round Up Motel & RV Park (257-2583), Fishtrap Lake Resort & Campground (235-2284), Sprague Lake Campground—showers (257-2864), fast-food stops, grocery store, cafe. *En route*: restaurant at the 14.4-mile mark.

Starting point: Sprague is located approximately 40 miles southwest of Spokane. From I-90, take the southbound Highway 23 exit. Turn right on N. 2nd Street. At the next intersection turn left onto B Street (unmarked). At the next stop sign, cross the unmarked street. Turn right on S. 2nd, go one block to C Street and the city park.

0: From the park, head back to B Street and **turn left**. Go one block, and **turn left** onto 1st Street (unmarked).

0.4: **Bear left** at the sign for Sprague Lake Campground. Begin making your way through a rocky basin of wetlands and sagebrush teaming with waterfowl, marmots, and other wildlife.

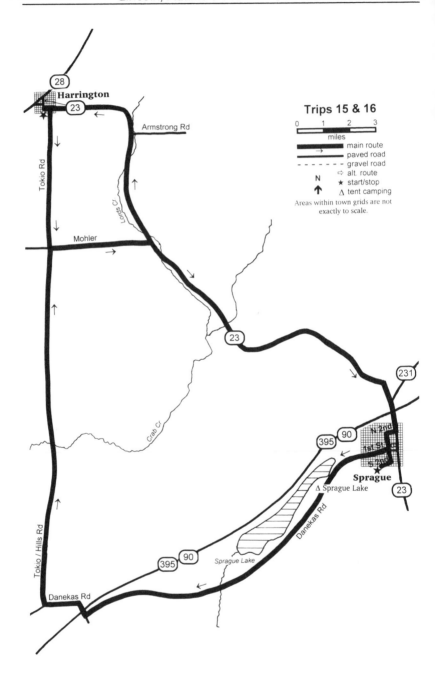

Trips 15 & 16

0 1 2 3
miles

main route
paved road
gravel road
⇨ alt. route
N
★ start/stop
↑ △ tent camping
Areas within town grids are not
exactly to scale.

14.4: Reach the junction with I-90, where you'll find the only *restaurant* on the route. Cross over I-90 and **bear left** onto Danekas Road (unmarked).

16.2: **Turn right** onto Hills Road (unmarked), following signs for Harrington and Davenport. Begin a series of small climbs.

22.5: Cross tree-lined Crab Creek. Continue through a series of moderate roller-coaster hills. BLM lands are to the left and right; trails are open to foot traffic.

29.8: **Turn right** onto Mohler Road (unmarked).

Alt. route: To add 13 miles to the trip, continue straight for 5 miles to Harrington—*cafes, grocery store, park*. From Harrington, take Highway 23 southbound through Lord's Valley and rejoin the main route at the 33.7-mile mark.

33.7: **Turn right** onto Highway 23, where traffic picks up but is still quite light. Soon you'll get a change of scenery as you enter an area irrigated by three creeks.

38.0: Cross Crab Creek. The surrounding cliffs provide habitat for hundreds of swallows that zoom overhead.

46.9: Highway 231 intersects from the left.

47.5: Continue straight at the junction with I-90.

47.9: **Turn right** onto N. 2nd Street.

48.1: **Turn left** at the brick church onto B Street (unmarked).

48.4: At the next stop sign, cross First Street (unmarked). Go one more block, **turn right** on S. 2nd, and return to the park.

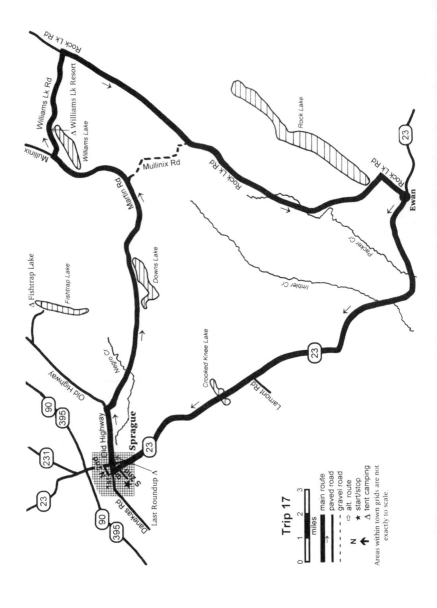

Trip 17

miles
0 1 2 3

N

main route
paved road
gravel road
alt. route
start/stop
tent camping

Areas within town grids are not exactly to scale.

17. Sprague - Williams Lake - Ewan

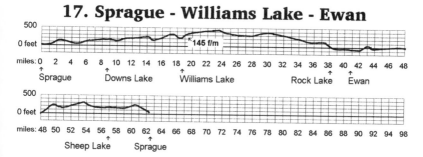

Miles: 62. This loop is ideal for cyclists looking for a long but not-too-strenuous ride. The trip begins in Sprague with a 10-mile stretch of rocky scabland. After leaving Williams Lake, where a restaurant makes a nice lunch stop, the scenery changes to open fields and woodlands for a few miles. Later, Rock Lake Road slices through the hilly wheat fields and takes you along Packer Creek, which provides life support for an impressive mile-long row of willow trees. Beyond Rock Lake and Ewan is a rather uneventful 22-mile stretch of Highway 23 through wheat fields and sagebrush. If you want to save the best till last, do the loop in the reverse direction. Traffic on the back roads is very light, and light to moderate on Highway 23. During the summer months, watch for RV's and boat trailers near the lakes.

Food/lodging/camping & starting point: *Sprague*: see trip 16. *Williams Lake*: Williams Lake Resort—camping, cabins, store, restaurant, swimming (509-235-2391).

    0: From the park, head back toward B Street.
 0.05: **Turn left** onto B Street.
  0.1: **Turn right** onto First Street (unmarked). Pass the Last Round-up Motel on the right. Continue straight ahead onto Old Highway (unmarked), making your way through rocky scablands.
  2.7: **Turn right**, following the signs to Downs Lake and Bunker's Resort. In 1.5 miles, pass a series of rocky embankments that serve as home to hundreds of swallows.
  8.7: A gravel road, leading .5 miles to Downs Lake, intersects from the right. As the main route skirts the lake basin, you pass a number of marshes and wetlands.
 13.7: **Bear left** onto Martin Road where Mullinix Road intersects from the right. Soon you'll get nice views into rocky basins.

17.4: **Turn right** onto Williams Lake Road just past two roads leading to Bunkers Resort.

18.7: Reach Williams Lake Resort—*restrooms, restaurant, store.*

19.7: Badger Lake Road, leading 1.5 miles to the lake, intersects from the left as the scenery changes to open fields and woodlands.

22.2: **Turn right** onto Rock Lake Road, which weaves in and out of the rolling wheat fields.

38.3: Reach the Rock Lake boat launch—*outhouses.*

40.8: Enter the community of Ewan—no services.

40.9: **Turn right** onto Highway 23, where traffic picks up a bit and the shoulder is come-and-go. The terrain is now a combination of rocky scabland, wheat fields, and grazing land.

57.0: Sheep Lake is to the left.

61.8: Enter Sprague.

62.2: **Turn left** onto an unmarked street, following the sign for the city center. One block later, **turn right** onto B Street (unmarked) following signs for the truck route.

62.3: **Turn left** onto 2nd Street and return to the park.

18. Wilbur - Wilson Creek Flood Channel

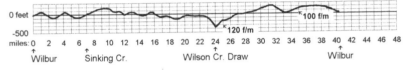

Miles: 40. Shallow roller-coaster hills through the wheat fields, scablands, and ice-age flood channels is the basic theme of this loop. The mile-long, 300-foot descent into the lush, green Wilson Creek channel is pure joy. Except for a couple of brief encounters with Highway 2, traffic ranges from very light to seemingly nonexistent.

Food/lodging/camping: *Wilbur:* Eight Bar-B Motel (**509**-647-2400), Settle Inn (467-2100), Crescent Oaks RV Park—tent sites, showers (647-5608), several drive-ins. *Almira:* two restaurants (639-0176, 639-2201).

Starting point: Wilbur is located 65 miles west of Spokane. To get to the city park, turn south on Division and go two blocks to Front Street.

0: From the park, head west on Front Street.

0.2: **Bear left** onto Highway 21 (unmarked) and begin a series of gentle roller-coasters through the wheat fields. Traffic is light.

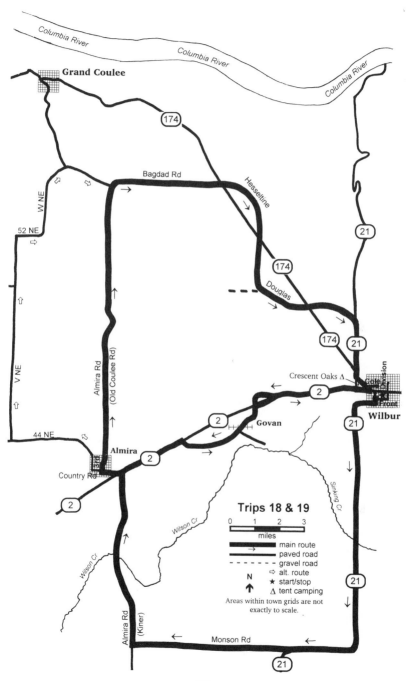

Columbia River

Columbia River

Columbia River

Grand Coulee

174

Bagdad Rd

Hesseltine

W NE

52 NE

174

Douglas

V NE

174 21

Almira Rd
(Old Coulee Rd)

Crescent Oaks Δ

21

Wilbur

Division
Front

2

44 NE

2 Govan

2

21

Almira

2

Country Rd

Trips 18 & 19

0   1   2   3

miles

■■■ main route
→ paved road
--- gravel road
⇨ alt. route
N ★ start/stop
↑ Δ tent camping

Areas within town grids are not
exactly to scale.

Wilson Cr

Wilson Cr

Sinking Cr

2

Almira Rd
(Kiner)

Monson Rd

21

6.9: Cross Sinking Creek, which flows through a shallow flood channel.

14.1: At the silos, **continue straight** onto Monson Road (unmarked), leaving Highway 21 as it veers left.

20.2: **Bear right** onto Almira/Kiner Road (unmarked) at a power substation and a series of silos. Watch for views of the snow-covered Cascades in the distance to the west.

23.0: The mile-long, rapid descent to Wilson Creek begins.

24.0: Reach the Wilson Creek flood channel—an oasis in a rocky basin. After a short stay, begin the moderate climb out. From here to Highway 2, you'll be riding through channeled scablands.

27.7: **Turn right** onto Highway 2.

Side trip: To visit the town of Almira, which has a tavern, two restaurants (limited hours) and a city park, turn left onto Highway 2. Take the next paved road to the right (about .3 miles) and follow it a half mile into town.

30.4: **Turn right** onto an unmarked road. This scenic side route to the community of Govan will spare you 3 miles on busy Highway 2.

32.6: **Bear left** at the unmarked paved road and cross the RR tracks.

33.0: **Turn right** onto Highway 2.

40.2: Reach Wilbur. **Turn right** onto Division and return to the park.

19. Wilbur North

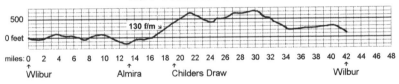

Miles: 42. This loop through the wheat fields begins in Wilbur and passes through the little town of Almira before making a long, moderate climb to the southern ridge of the Grand Coulee. Traffic on the majority of the route is very light.

Food/lodging/camping & starting point: see trip 18.

0: From the park, head north on Division.

0.1: **Turn left** onto Highway 2.

4.3: **Bear right** onto the unmarked paved road. This side route will save you 5 miles of travel on Highway 2.

5.5: Cross Highway 2 and continue straight.

66

7.5: After crossing the RR tracks, **bear right** at the Y.

8.5: On a clear day, you can see the Cascades in the distance.

9.7: **Turn left** onto Highway 2, where pavement is smooth and shoulders are wide.

12.6: **Turn right**, following the signs for Almira.

13.3: **Turn right** at the junction of Main and Third and cross the RR tracks. Soon you'll begin an eight-mile, moderate ascent through the wheat fields.

> *Side trip*: Continue straight ahead to Almira—*cafe*.
>
> *Alt. route*: To add 7 miles to the loop, after crossing the tracks, turn left onto Country Road and then take the next right (.1 miles later). Four and a half miles later, turn right onto V NE. Eight miles later, the road first veers right and becomes 52 NE and then left, becoming W NE. Four miles later (at the stop sign) turn right and rejoin the main route at the 25.1-mile mark.

25.1: **Bear right** onto Bagdad Road (unmarked).

26.1: Reach Grand Coulee Grange, which sports 2 *outhouses*.

27.7: Reach the remnants of an old, stone structure. The remaining 8-foot wall provides some shade from mid-morning sun. Stop a moment and absorb the absolute peace and quiet.

29.6: At the junction with Highway 174, continue straight onto Hesseltine Road (unmarked). On a clear day, there is a seemingly infinite view to the east.

32.8: Cross Highway 174 once again.

34.8: **Bear left** onto Douglas Road (unmarked).

36.9: Cross Highway 174 for the third time.

39.4: **Turn right** onto Highway 21 (unmarked).

41.4: **Bear left** where Highway 174 joins Highway 21.

41.7: Bear left just past the golf course.

42.3: Bear left onto Cole Street and parallel Highway 2.

41.9: Turn right onto Division, cross Highway 2, and return to the city park.

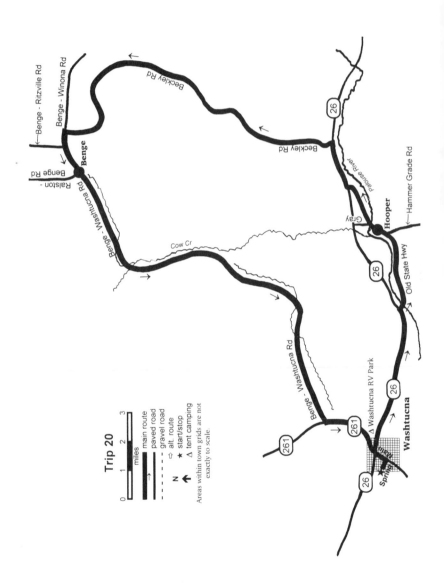

20. Washtucna - Palouse River - Staley Coulee

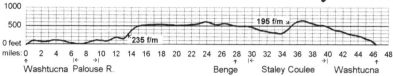

Miles: 47. A wide range of scenery awaits the cyclist on this fairly long loop comprised of a lush, irrigated river valley, rocky fields with mesas and other geological formations, a rugged coulee and, of course, wheat fields. A glance at the elevation profile reveals that while the two major hills are fairly steep, they are less than two miles long. Also included are extensive level sections and long, down-hill cruises. Except for 7 miles on Highway 26, where volumes remain quite tolerable, and a 3-mile stint on Highway 261, traffic is extremely light. While there are no restaurants on the route, there is a small grocery store just outside Hooper (9.5-mile mark) and another in Benge (28-mile mark).

Food/lodging/camping: *Washtucna*: motel & RV park (**509**-646-3352), two restaurants (646-3245, 646-3262). *Benge*: grocery store.

Starting point: Washtucna is 50 miles west of Colfax at the junction of Highway 26 and Highway 261. To get to the park, head south on 261, go 6 blocks, and turn right onto Spring Street.

0: Return to Highway 261 (Main Street) and **turn left**.

0.7: **Turn right** onto Highway 26, which has smooth pavement, a wide shoulder, and moderate traffic. Begin making your way through rocky sagebrush fields.

5.9: **Turn right** onto an unmarked, paved road, which leads to Hooper. In a quarter mile you'll cross the Palouse River and begin making your way into the lush, green Palouse Basin.

9.1: Hammer Grade Road intersects left and right.

> 9.3: *Side trip*: Turn left to visit the sleepy, community of Hooper. No services, but there are large, public lawns lined with tall shade trees—a very pleasant place to rest or fill *water* bottles.

9.5: Gray Road intersects from the left. At the junction you'll find a small grocery store with a shaded lawn and table.

11.3: **Turn right** on Highway 26, returning to sagebrush and mesas.

13.0: **Turn left** onto Beckley Road (unmarked), which leads to Benge. Begin a fairly steep incline into an area of mesas, ponds, and wondrous geological formations. Traffic is virtually non-existent.

15.0: Reach the crest of the hill. In the next level 7 miles, as hawks circle overhead, the rocky topography gradually gives way to wheat fields.

24.0: Reach the peak of a short hill, where the view overlooks fields of mesas and other rock formations.

26.6: **Turn left** onto Benge-Winona Road.

27.1: Benge-Ritsville Road intersects from the right.

27.8: Enter the community of Benge. A small school on the right features shade trees, a sprawling lawn, and *water*.

28.0: Ralston-Benge Road intersects from the right, leading to Ralston, Ritzville, and Lind. At this junction there is a small grocery store; across the street is a small park with a covered picnic table. Continue straight on what is now Benge-Washtucna Road.

29.0: Cow Creek creates an isolated habitat for herons, rabbits and other wildlife.

30.0: Mesas once again embellish the fields as you begin the descent into scenic Staley Coulee.

31.7: Reach a one-lane RR underpass—watch for **rough roadway**.

32.5: A roadside attraction provides history on this road's origins as a pioneer trail.

43.4: **Turn left** onto unmarked Highway 261, where traffic is light and there is a narrow shoulder.

45.7: At the junction with Highway 26, continue straight into Washtucna.

46.4: **Turn right** onto Spring Street and return to the park.

21. Connell - Snake River - Devil's Canyon

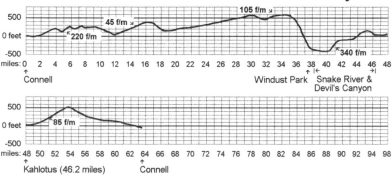

Miles: 63.5. This is definitely not a trip for the inexperienced, under-conditioned, or inadequately equipped. Quality brakes and cables in proper working order are absolutely mandatory for the steep, winding, 5-mile descent to the Snake River. The uphill stretches are fairly reasonable, the longer ones being moderate in grade and the steeper ones relatively short in duration. However, total elevation gain is considerably greater than hillgraph confesses, due to countless, shallow hills. Scenery on the first half of the trip alternates between hilly wheat fields and sagebrush fields with occasional sections of rockier topography. Traffic in the first half is very light—you have the road to yourself a great deal of the time. After the descent to the Snake River and Highway 263, where Windust Park makes a welcome rest stop, traffic picks up. During harvest season, be on the watch for tractor-trailer combinations making their way through narrow Devil's Canyon. Beyond Kahlotus, on Highway 260, the scenery is once again a combination of wheat fields, sagebrush, and mesas. The increase in traffic on 260 is offset by smooth pavement and generous shoulders.

Food/lodging/camping: *Connell*: two motels (**509**-234-2081, 234-8811). Several restaurants. *Kahlotus* has a small grocery store.

Starting point: Connell is approximately 40 miles south of Ritzville, near the intersection of Highway 395 and Highway 260. From 395, take 260 westbound. A half mile later, turn right onto Columbia. In another half mile, just as you reach the old, historic section of town, take a right onto Birch Street and go two blocks to Pioneer Park.

0.0: Return to Columbia and **turn left**.
0.9: **Turn left** onto Highway 260.

71

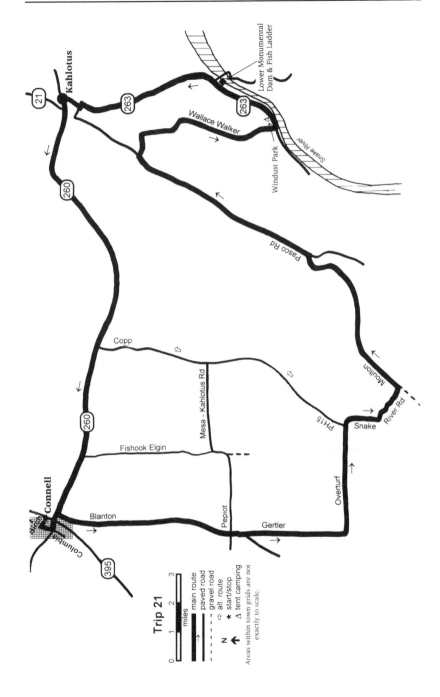

Lower Monumental
Dam & Fish Ladder

Kahlotus

21

263

263

Wallace Walker

Windust Park

Snake River

260

Pasco Rd

Copp

Moulton

River Rd

Mesa - Kahlotus Rd

PH15

Snake

Fishook Elgin

Connell

Overturf

260

Blanton

Pepiot

Gertler

Columbia

395

Trip 21

miles
0   1   2   3

main route
paved road
gravel road
⇨ alt. route
★ start/stop
△ tent camping

N ←

Areas within town grids are not
exactly to scale.

1.3: **Turn right** onto Blanton and begin a moderate climb, followed by a series of roller-coaster hills.

2.4: Havlina Road intersects from the left.

7.9: **Bear left** onto Gertler Road just beyond the junction with Pepiot Road.

11.6: **Turn left** onto Overturf Road.

15.3: **Bear right** onto Snake River Road (unmarked) immediately after Road PH15 intersects from the left.

> *Short cut*: Road PH15 (marked Coop at the other end) cuts a narrow channel through the wheat fields north to Highway 260.

18.2: **Turn left** onto Moulton Road.

19.6: Harper Road intersects from the left.

24.5: **Turn left** onto Pasco Road.

31.4: **Turn right** on Wallace-Walker Road—a winding path through endless, hilly wheat fields.

33.5: At the edge of the gorge, you get a terrific view down to the Snake River. ***Caution***: shortly, you begin a five-mile descent through Wilson Canyon. At the steepest point, you lose 700 feet in one mile. There are several ***blind turns.*** Check brakes and cables before proceeding!

37.6: **Turn left** onto Highway 263 at the bottom of the descent. Straight across the highway is Windust Park—*water, restrooms.*

40.4: Reach Lower Monumental Lock and Dam and begin a steep, but short, ascent into Devil's Canyon.

45.8: **Turn right**, following Highway 263 to Kahlotus.

46.5: **Turn left** onto Highway 260. At this junction find a small *store.*

46.6: Highway 21 intersects from the right.

62.7: **Turn right** onto Columbia after crossing Highway 395.

63.5: **Turn right** onto Birch and return to the park.

Looking west to Thompson Ridge (trip 29)

McNitt Road, running through the hills above the Kettle River (trip 29)

6

Stevens & Pend Oreille Counties

One of Washington's best-kept secrets is the northeastern corner of the state. The back roads in this area offer marvelous scenery, passing through rural farmlands and forests, along the shores of lakes and rivers—including the upper Columbia, the Pend Oreille River, Waitts Lake, and Sullivan Lake—and over the mountains of the Colville National Forest.

Despite the relative ruggedness of the area, a couple of the routes are quite easy, particularly trips 22 and 23. By contrast, trip 28 begins with the steepest climb in this entire guide. There are also significant climbs on most of the other trips described in this section. But the rewards are great; besides the exhilaration of making it to the top, the steep climbs are followed by long, gradual, down-hill cruises over back roads that wind their way through scenic valleys and forests.

Logging is the primary industry in northeastern Washington. Keep an eye out for trucks and related equipment.

Trips:

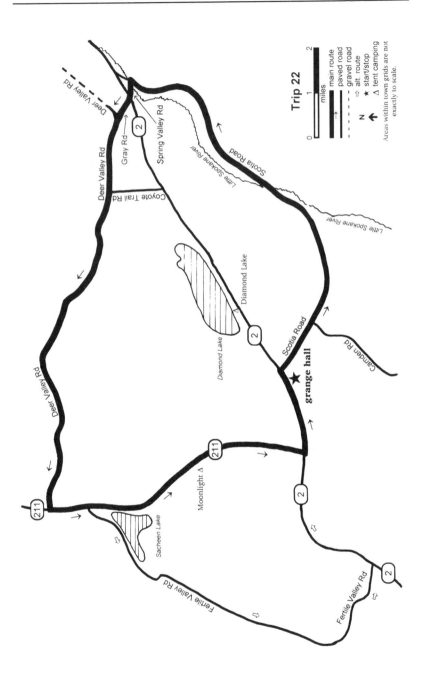

Trip 22

22. Scotia Valley - Deer Valley - Sacheen Lake

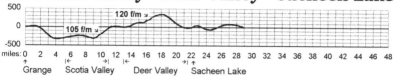

Miles: 29-37. Located just 30 miles north of the junction of Highway 395 and Highway 2, this low-key, scenic loop offers a sure cure for Spokane cyclists suffering from BRS (Busy Road Syndrome). The trip begins with a descent into Scotia Valley, where the county road parallels the Little Spokane River for seven miles, traveling through forested areas, open fields, rural farmland, and wetlands. A moderate climb into Deer Valley after crossing Highway 2 brings more of the same. Traffic picks up after reaching Highway 211, but remains quite tolerable.

Food/lodging/camping: Moonlight RV Park (**509**-447-5463), Diamond Lake Resort (447-4474). At the 21.4-mile mark, there is a small market with a deli & bakery.

Starting point: On Highway 2, about 30 miles north of the junction with Highway 395, North Shore Road intersects from the left. Immediately afterwards, park at the Diamond Lake Grange Hall on the right.

   0: **Turn right** onto Highway 2.
  0.2: **Turn right** onto Scotia Road and begin a moderate descent into the valley.
  1.6: Camden Road intersects from the right and left.
 10.0: **Turn left** onto Spring Valley Road and begin a short climb to Highway 2.
 10.5: Cross Highway 2 and continue onto Gray Road.
 11.3: **Turn left** onto Deer Valley Road.
 12.9: Coyote Trail Road intersects left and right.
 20.8: **Turn left** onto Highway 211, where traffic varies from fairly light to moderate.
 21.4: Reach a deli-store-bakery with a couple of picnic tables off to the side—*restrooms, water.*
     21.7: *Alt. route:* To add about 8 miles to the trip, turn right onto Fertile Valley Road and follow it for 9 miles through scenic

Fertile Valley to Highway 2. Turn left onto Highway 2 and rejoin the main route at the 27.1-mile mark.

23.5: Reach moonlight RV Park—*tent sites, showers.*

27.1: **Turn left** onto Highway 2, which has smooth pavement and a five-foot shoulder.

28.6: **Turn right** at the grange hall.

23. Chewelah - Waitts Lake

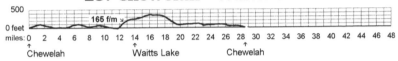

Miles: 27-39. With the exception of a moderate climb to Waitts Lake, this loop is a virtually flat exploration of the east and west extremes of the lower Colville Valley. Most of the trip is through rolling farmland and wetlands surrounded by forested hills—spectacular scenery the entire way. Both the town of Valley and the Waitts Lake area offer options for a lunch break. An out-and-back side trip through Long Prairie allows for an additional 12 miles. Traffic is very light most of the way, with the exception of two brief stints on Highway 395. Traffic on Waitts Lake Road varies, depending on the time of year and day of week—the lake is a popular recreation area.

Food/lodging/camping: *Chewelah*: 49'er Motel and RV Park (**509**-935-8664), Nordlig Motel (935-6704), restaurants and cafes. *Valley*: general store, tavern with food (937-2503), cafe (937-2111). *Waitts Lake*: Winona Beach Resort (937-2231), Waitts Lake Resort & Motel (937-2400) Silver Beach Resort (937-2811), stores, restaurants.

Starting point: Chewelah is located approximately 50 miles north of Spokane on Highway 395. Find the city park on the east side of Highway 395 at the north end of Chewelah.

0: From the park, head east on Lincoln.

0.5: **Turn right** onto Ehorn.

0.7: **Turn left** onto Flowery Trail.

1.1: **Turn right** onto Cottonwood Creek Road and begin making your way through pastures, trees, wetlands, and farmland along the east side of the Colville Valley.

6.0: **Turn right** onto Hafer Road at the yield sign.

7.3: **Turn left** onto busy Highway 395. (Stay tuned—you're only here for a quarter mile.)

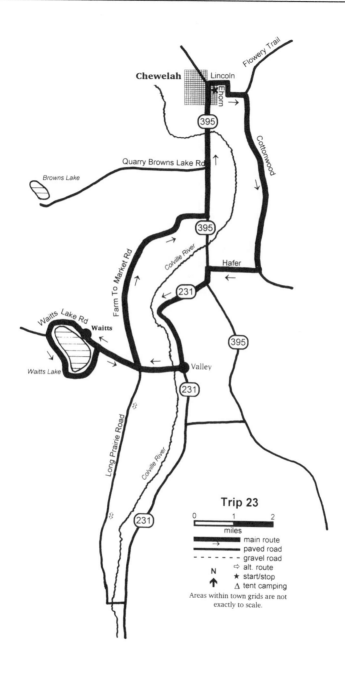

Trip 23

0 1 2
miles

━━━━━━ main route
→ paved road
- - - - - gravel road
⇨ alt. route
★ start/stop
△ tent camping

Areas within town grids are not exactly to scale.

7.6: **Turn right** onto Highway 231.

10.7: Enter the town of Valley.

10.9: Continue straight at the first paved road intersecting from the right and continue into town on Highway 231.

11.0: **Turn right**, following signs to Waitts Lake. In the next few blocks, Valley offers *food, a general store, and cafe.*

11.1: Cross the RR tracks and continue westbound through open farmland, watching for RV's and vehicles hauling boats to the lake.

12.3: Continue straight ahead and up the hill as Farm to Market Road and Long Prairie Road intersect from the right and left.

> *Side trip*: To add 12 level miles to the trip, turn left onto Long Prairie Road, follow it to Highway 231, turn around, and return to the 12.3-mile point.

13.7: Waitts Lake Road intersects from the left. A number of resorts, beaches and restaurants lie ahead.

15.3: **Bear left** where an unmarked, paved road intersects from the right and continue around the lake.

18.1: **Bear right** where Waitts Lake Road South intersects from the right.

19.5: **Turn left** onto Farm to Market Road and begin making your way through rural farmland along the west side of the Colville Valley.

24.9: **Turn left** onto Highway 395. The three-mile stint on this busy highway is made tolerable by smooth, wide shoulders.

28.4: **Turn right** onto Lincoln (at the Parkside restaurant), and return to the city park.

24. Addy - Blue Creek

Miles: 15. This loop around Rieckers Mountain begins with a moderate, five-mile climb through the forest, levels out for four miles, and then rolls down through a scenic valley on the way back to Addy. Traffic is very light.

Food/lodging/camping: The closest lodging is in Chewelah, about 10 minutes south. In Addy, a mini-market on Highway 395 and another in town offer sandwiches and snacks.

Starting point: Addy is located approximately 60 miles north of Spokane on Highway 395. At the *Old Schoolhouse Trading Post*, head southwest on Addy-Main Road. At the T, turn right onto Addy-Gifford Road and park along the shoulder just before the RR tracks.

- 0: Continue on Addy-Gifford Road, crossing the RR tracks and the Colville River.
- 0.9: Marble Valley Basin Road intersects from the right.
- 1.5: **Bear left**, staying with Addy-Gifford Road, where Swiss Valley Road intersects from the right. Begin a moderate climb.
- 6.2: **Turn left** onto Blue Creek Road and cross Stensgar Creek.
- 6.7: Bluecreek Road swings 90 degrees to the left. For the next four miles the route is fairly level.
- 10.0: The descent steepens, providing a scenic roll through the valley as you chase Blue Creek down to the Colville Valley.
- 11.3: **Turn left** onto Zimmer Road.
- 14.1: **Turn right** onto Addy-Gifford Road.
- 15.1: Cross the Colville River and the tracks and return to the start point.

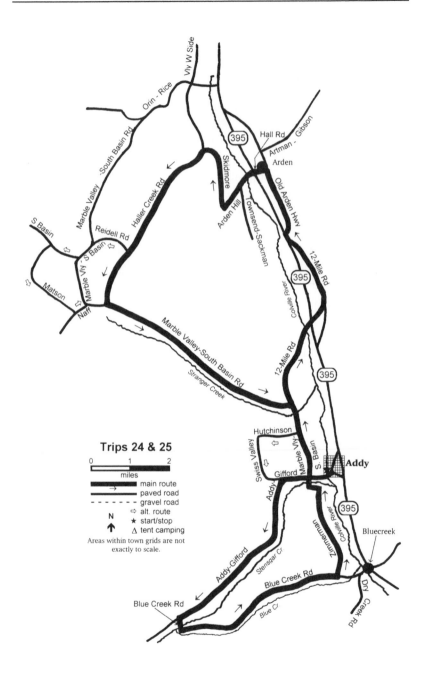

Trips 24 & 25

0   1   2
miles

━━━ main route
→   paved road
--- gravel road
⇨   alt. route
★   start/stop
△   tent camping

Areas within town grids are not
exactly to scale.

25. Addy - Marble Valley Basin

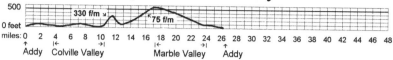

Miles: 26-32. Two long, flat valleys, scenery ranging from rural farmland to peaceful forests, very light traffic, and only one mile of serious climbing, make this one of the best loops around. An optional side loop (6.2 miles) and the ability to combine this loop with trip 22 for a total of nearly 50 miles allow for tailoring to individual needs.

Food/lodging/camping/starting point: see trip 24.

0: Continue on Addy-Gifford Road, crossing the RR tracks and the Colville River.

0.8: **Turn right** onto Marble Valley Basin Road and begin making your way through open fields and pastures.

2.0: Hutchinson Road intersects from the left.

2.9: **Turn right** onto 12-mile Road.

5.4: Cross Highway 395, continuing on 12-mile Road.

5.5: **Turn left** at the stop sign at the unmarked intersection, continuing on 12-mile Road.

6.0: Slide Creek Road intersects from the right.

7.8: **Turn right** onto Highway 395.

8.0: **Turn right** onto Old Arden Highway (unmarked at the intersection).

9.7: **Turn left** onto Hall Road.

10.0: Cross Highway 395 onto Arden Hill Road. Cross the Colville River and begin a one-mile, steep climb.

10.4: **Bear right** where Townsend-Sackman Road intersects from the left.

11.2: **Turn right** onto Skidmore and coast down the other side of the hill.

12.8: After a 90-degree swing to the left, cross Haller Creek.

13.0: **Turn left** onto Haller Creek Road, which makes its way through the forest, following Haller Creek.

16.3: Reidell Creek Road intersects from the right.

> *Alt. route:* To add 6.2 miles and a couple hundred extra feet of elevation gain, turn right onto Reidell Creek Road. In about a mile, bear left onto Marble Valley-South Basin Road.

A half mile later, bear right at the Y. At the next Y (less than a mile later) bear left onto Matson. Two miles later, turn left onto Naff and then right onto Marble Valley-South Basin.

17.1: At the T, **turn left** onto Marble Valley-South Basin Road and begin a long descent through Marble Valley, following Stranger Creek on its way to the Colville River. Scenery includes rural farmland, pastures, marshes, and forest—all at the base of Dunn Mountain.

23.6: 12-mile Road intersects from the left.

24.5: Hutchinson Road intersects from the right.

Alt. route: To bypass Addy and proceed to trip 22, turn right onto Hutchinson. About 1.5 miles later, turn right onto Addy-Gifford Road, joining trip 22 at the 1.5-mile mark.

25.6: **Turn left** onto Addy-Gifford Road.

26.4: Cross the Colville River and the RR tracks and return to the starting point.

26. Colville - Northport

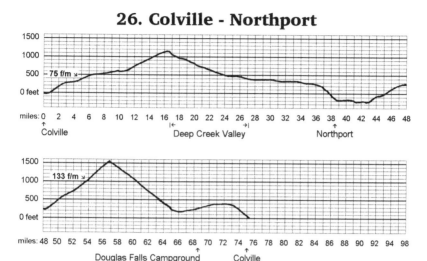

Miles: 75 (114 with trip 25). This scenic trip begins with a moderate climb into Mill Creek Valley. Another long but moderate climb brings you into Deep Creek Valley. Here, you are rewarded with a 10-mile, slightly downward cruise through open fields, pastures, and forests, while the mountains of the Colville National Forest gracefully slope into the valley. After leaving the valley, a steep plunge puts you in Northport. The trip back begins with a 15-mile climb through the forest. After reaching the peak, you immediately begin a 10-mile roll down the other side. The final eight-mile stretch is fairly level.

This is a long, challenging ride. Though traffic is quite light, watch out for occasional logging trucks and related equipment.

To expand this loop into a three-day trip, spend day one getting to Northport, do the Northport loop on day two, and return to Colville on day three.

Starting point: Colville is located 75 miles north of Spokane on Highway 395. From northbound 395, at the south end of town, at the signal just past McDonalds, turn right onto Hawthorne. Two blocks later, turn left onto Elm, and find parking at the city park.

Food/lodging/camping: *Colville:* Benny's Inn (**509**-684-2517), Downtown Motel (684-2565), Comfort Inn (684-2010), Douglas Falls Campground (684-7010). Several restaurants, cafes, fast-food stops. *Northport:* Clark's Motel (732-4495), saloon & eatery (732-6638), cafe (732-8874), laundry/showers.

85

0: From the park, head north on Elm.

0.8: **Turn right** onto Sixth, following the bike route.

1.1: **Bear left** onto Hoffstetter.

1.2: **Turn right** onto East Seventh.

1.8: **Turn left** at the stop sign onto Alladin (unmarked), where the shoulder varies from adequate to poor and the traffic is light. Begin making your way through a rural area with open pastures and wooded hills. Landmark: a mile later, you'll pass a cemetery on the left.

3.6: **Bear right** as Douglas Falls Road intersects from the left. The shoulder narrows.

17.0: Reach the peak of the first climb.

19.6: Rocky Creek Road (gravel) intersects from the right as you enter Deep Creek Valley. Alladin Mountain is to the right. The community of Alladin is one mile ahead—no services.

26.4: South Fork Mill Creek Road (gravel) intersects from the right as you enter an enchanting stretch where the surrounding mountains and ridges slope down into the valley from all sides.

27.8: **Bear left** where Deep Lake-Boundary Road (unmarked) intersects from the right.

31.1: You're at the base of Stoddard Mountain.

36.1: Begin the steep, winding descent into Northport. On the way down, the Columbia River comes into view.

37.8: **Bear right** where a paved road intersects from the left.

38.4: **Turn left** onto Highway 25 (Center Street). On this eight-mile section of Highway 25, you'll find marginal shoulders and fairly light traffic.

> *Side trip*: Turn right to visit Northport—*restaurants, motels, showers.*

38.9: Northport School is on the left as you head out of town. A little later, you'll get nice views of the Columbia River and Hubbard Ridge on your right.

45.7: **Turn left** onto Clugston-Onion Road, where the shoulder varies from marginal to non-existent and traffic is quite light. Begin a 15-mile, moderate ascent into the Colville National Forest.

50.8: A *gas station-mini mart* on the right marks the halfway point of this climb.

56.4: Reach the peak and begin the long cruise down the other side.

64.8: **Bear right** as Douglas Falls Road (gravel) intersects from the left.

65.0: **Turn left** onto Williams Lake Road, where traffic picks up for a few minutes.

66.2: **Turn left** onto Gillette Road.

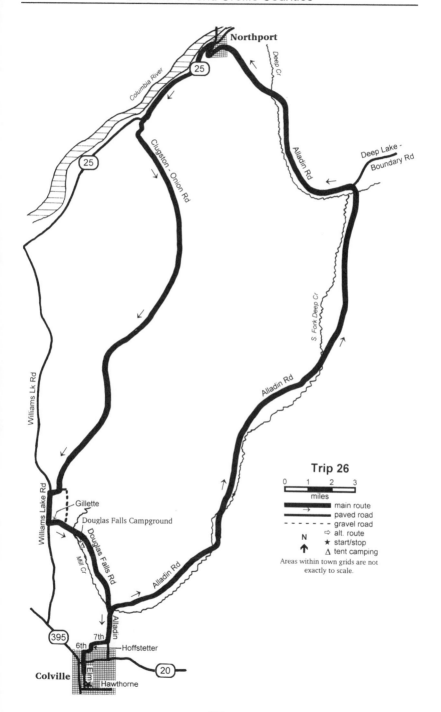

Trip 26

0 1 2 3
miles

main route
paved road
gravel road
alt. route
★ start/stop
△ tent camping

Areas within town grids are not
exactly to scale.

66.7: **Turn right** onto Douglas Falls Road, which is paved at this point.

68.5: Reach Douglas Falls Campground.

71.4: **Turn right** onto Alladin Road (unmarked).

73.1: **Turn right** onto unmarked East Seventh Street and follow the bike route. (Laundry Street is to the left at this intersection.)

73.8: **Turn left** onto Hoffstetter.

73.9: **Turn right** onto Sixth Street.

74.2: **Turn left** onto Elm and go one mile to the park.

27. Northport - Cedar Lake - Deep Lake

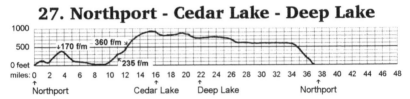

Miles: 38. This loop is for experienced, seasoned cyclists only. The trip begins with a steep, narrow, winding ascent along the upper Columbia River, where cyclists must cope with logging trucks and RV's. After reaching the peak and rolling down the other side, things mellow out for awhile. Four miles down the road is a five-mile ascent that begins fairly steeply and then graduates to 360 ft./mi. for most of the last three miles. Once the peak is crested, the payoff begins: 20 miles of gradual descent, following first Cedar Creek and then Deep Creek on a lightly traveled road that meanders through forests, open fields, rural farmland, and lakes. In addition to a small store at the 10-mile mark, during the summer you'll find two small grocery stores open near Deep Lake—a popular recreation spot. See trip 24 for details on combining this loop with the Colville Loop.

Food/lodging/camping: *Northport*: see trip 26. At the 5.0-mile mark: Homeland RV Park and Campground (**509**-732-4367). *Deep Lake*: Wilderness West Resort (732-4263).

Starting point: Northport is located 50 miles north of Colville on Highway 395. To get to the city park from northbound Highway 25, go to the north end of town, turn right on Northport-Boundary Road, take an immediate left onto the park access road, pass several industrial buildings, and descend to the park. The mileage log begins at the junction of the park-access road and Northport-Boundary Road.

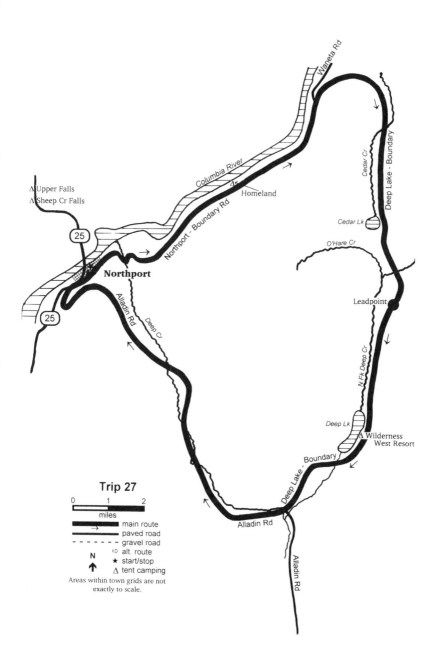

Trip 27

0   1   2
miles
⟶ main route
    paved road
- - - - - gravel road
⇨ alt. route
N   ★ start/stop
↑   △ tent camping
Areas within town grids are not
exactly to scale.

0: **Turn left** onto Northport-Boundary Road. *Caution:* During the first 3 miles, the shoulder is quite poor at times. Keep an eye on the mirror and be prepared for short-notice encounters with logging trucks and RV's on this steep, winding ascent.

2.9: After cresting the peak, you get views of the Columbia and Mitchell Mountain to the right as you roll down the other side.

5.0: Reach *Homeland RV Park & Campground*. Things settle down considerably as you move along the Columbia River Valley.

6.8: The road narrows and shoulders disappear as you enter a brief, winding section.

9.8: **Bear right** where Waneta Road intersects from the left. There is a small *store* here. A bit later, you'll get magnificent views into the upper Columbia River, as you begin a five-mile ascent that steepens after 2 miles and then backs off some for the final mile.

16.1: Cedar Lake is to the right.

18.4: Enter the community of Leadpoint—no services. The long, flat section continues.

21.8: Reach Deep Lake and Wilderness West Resort—*camping, store, swimming*. Another small store is 1.5 miles ahead.

25.9: **Bear right** onto Alladin Road and continue a gentle descent between Lime Creek Mountain and Stoddard Mountain.

35.0: Begin the steep, winding descent into Northport as the Columbia River comes into view.

36.7: **Bear right** where a paved road intersects from the left.

37.3: **Turn right** at the stop sign onto Highway 25, passing through Northport.

37.5: **Turn right** onto Northport-Boundary Road, take an immediate left onto the park access road, and return to the city park.

28. Columbia River Out-and-Back

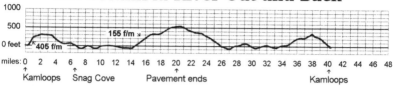

Miles: 40.2. After testing your mettle against a very steep hill in the first mile, followed by a more moderate hill in the second mile, you are rewarded with a gorgeous cruise along the west shore of the Columbia River. Beyond Snag Cove, the lightly traveled road is often sandwiched between the banks of the river to the east and the rocky cliffs to the west. If you're watchful, you'll likely see a bald eagle or two soaring overhead or perched in a snag. After the ten-mile mark, the road moves up and away from the water and makes its way through forests and open fields, the hills of the Colville National Forest providing a continuous backdrop.

Food/lodging/camping: There are no services along the route. Seven miles back on Highway 395, in Kettle Falls, you will find the Kettle Falls Inn (**509**-738-6514) and several restaurants. A mile north of the starting point on Highway 395 is Whispering Pines Campground (738-2593)—hot showers.

Starting point: Seven miles north of Kettle Falls on Highway 395, turn right onto unmarked Northport-Flat Creek Road, following the signs for Kamloops Campground. Several hundred feet later, turn left on the campground access road and find parking along the shoulder. To avoid the steep hill at the beginning of the trip, drive to Snag Cove Campground and start from there.

   0: **Turn left** onto Northport-Flat Creek Road. After a rough RR crossing, the big climb begins.

  1.1: Lake Roosevelt comes into view at the top of the first hill as the road passes through pine trees and open fields.

  2.0: Reach the peak of the second climb. After descending the other side, the route is fairly level for ten miles.

  6.6: Reach Snag Cove Campground—*seasonal water, outhouses.* For the next 3.5 miles, the Columbia River will be immediately to the right.

10.0: The road moves up and away from the river.

91

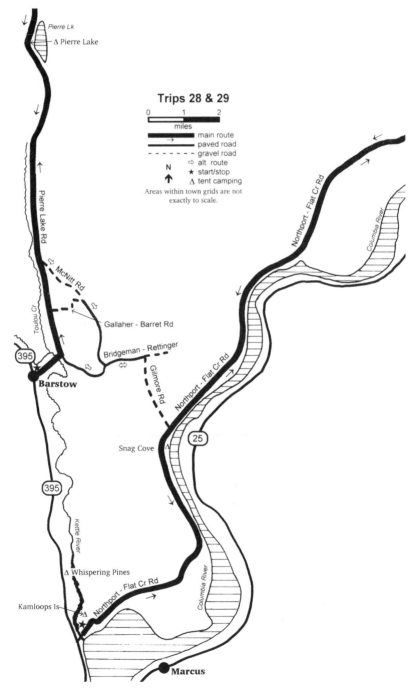

Pierre Lk
Δ Pierre Lake

Trips 28 & 29

0   1   2
miles

━━━━━━ main route
→   paved road
- - - - - gravel road
⇨   alt. route
N   ★ start/stop
↑   Δ tent camping

Areas within town grids are not
exactly to scale.

Pierre Lake Rd

Northport - Flat Cr Rd

Columbia River

McNitt Rd

Toulou Cr

Gallaher - Barret Rd

Bridgeman - Rettinger

Gilmore Rd

Northport - Flat Cr Rd

395

Barstow

395

Snag Cove Δ

25

Kettle River

Δ Whispering Pines

Kamloops Is

Northport - Flat Cr Rd

Columbia River

★ Δ

Marcus

13.1: A dirt road leads to an undeveloped National Park site along the water. A mile later, a moderate, but persistent, climb begins as the road moves away from the river and into the forest.

20.1: Reach the end of the paved road and the turn-around point.

29. Barstow - Kettle River - Pierre Lake

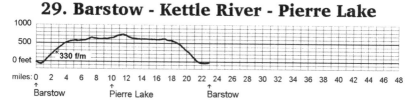

Miles: 23-28. This out-and-back trip (an optional loop requires a 2-mile stretch on a gravel road) moves through pastures, fields, and pine forests on its way to a scenic mountain lake in the Colville National Forest. After a steep climb up from the Kettle River, the rest of the trip is only slightly uphill. An optional loop offers nice views of surrounding valleys and mountains, including Thompson Ridge to the west. Traffic is very light.

Food/lodging/camping: Pierre Lake Campground (509-684-7010). See trip 28 for details on motels and restaurants in Kettle Falls, 13 miles south. Ten miles north, in the town of Orient, is the People Place (684-5644)—restaurant, showers, small grocery store.

Starting point: Thirteen miles north of Kettle Falls on Highway 395, you'll reach the Barstow General Store—*groceries, water, and restrooms.* Turn right just past the store, where signs indicate 12 miles to Pierre Lake and Kelly Hill. There are restrooms and shoulder parking immediately to the left.

0: Head east on the unmarked road you turned onto from the highway. At .1 miles, intersecting from the right is the Barstow Bridge Spur, which turns to gravel on the way to a large, undeveloped parcel of public land along the Kettle River—a pleasant place to visit.

1.0: After crossing the Kettle River, **turn left** onto Pierre Lake Road, which has coarse pavement, no shoulder, and very light traffic, and begin a steep climb. To the west are views of the Kettle River Valley.

2.3: Gallaher-Barret Road (gravel) intersects from the right as the ascent eases considerably.

3.8: McNitt Road (gravel) intersects from the right.

9.3: Reach the south end of Pierre Lake.

10.1: Reach Pierre Lake Campground.

11.5: Pierre Lake Road turns to gravel. Turn around, take in views of the lake, nestled at the base of Hungry Hill, and follow the pavement back to Barstow.

> *Alt. route*: (5 additional miles). If you can handle a 2-mile section of hard-packed gravel, on the way back (at 19.3 miles), **turn left** onto McNitt Road and begin a moderate ascent, getting great views into the valley below. At the Y, **bear left** where Gallaher-Barret Road intersects from the right. In another mile (22.0), the road leading to Pia Mission (a peaceful, hundred-year-old cemetery) intersects from the right. About a mile later, **bear left** on Bridgeman-Rettinger and follow it for another mile to the end of the pavement. Turn around and prepare for an exhilarating roll down to the Kettle River. Be prepared in advance to **bear left** in a mile or so where McNitt Road intersects from the right. Nice views of Thompson Ridge are to the west. At the bottom of the hill, cross the bridge and rejoin the main route back to Barstow.

30. Ione - Sullivan Lake

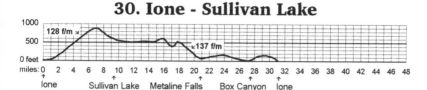

Miles: 31. This scenic loop through the Colville National Forest begins with a seven-mile, moderate climb through pastures, forest, and rural areas. After ten miles, you reach Sullivan Lake, nestled at the base of Hall Mountain. Here you'll find a number of campgrounds, a seasonal store, and other attractions. The 4-mile, flat ride along the lake's west shore offers some of the best scenery in the area. After leaving the lake, you roll 500 feet down to Metaline Falls—a good place to stop for lunch. The next five, mostly level miles offer views into the Pend Oreille Valley and Box Canyon. Four miles later, you're back in Ione. In the off season, you'll encounter very little traffic.

Food/lodging/camping: *Ione:* Pend Oreille Inn (**509**-442-3418), Ione Motel & RV (442-3213), Plaza Motel & Cafe (442-3534), Box Canyon Resort (800-676-8883). *Metaline Falls:* three restaurants (446-2447, 446-4806, 446-4234), Circle Motel (446-4343), Mt. Linton Motel (446-2238). *Sullivan Lake:* three NFS campgrounds (446-7500).

Starting point: Ione is located approximately 20 miles south of the Canadian border on Highway 31. At milepost 4, in the center of Ione, turn east onto an unmarked street and go two blocks to the city park.

   0: Return to Highway 31. **Turn left** and head south.
 1.2: **Turn left** onto Elizabeth Avenue.
 1.5: **Bear left** onto Sullivan Lake Road (also marked Road 9345) where LeClerc Road intersects from the right. Begin a moderate, seven-mile ascent through pastures, forests, hills, and rural homes.
 7.6: Road 1935 (gravel) intersects from the right.
 8.7: Hall Mountain rises to the sky straight ahead.
 9.3: *Noisy Creek Campground* is on the right.
 9.4: Sullivan Lake is to the right, at the base of Hall Mountain.
13.5: After crossing the creek that flows out of Lake Sullivan, reach *West Sullivan Campground* and Sullivan Lake Ranger Station. At this point the road leaves the shore of the lake.

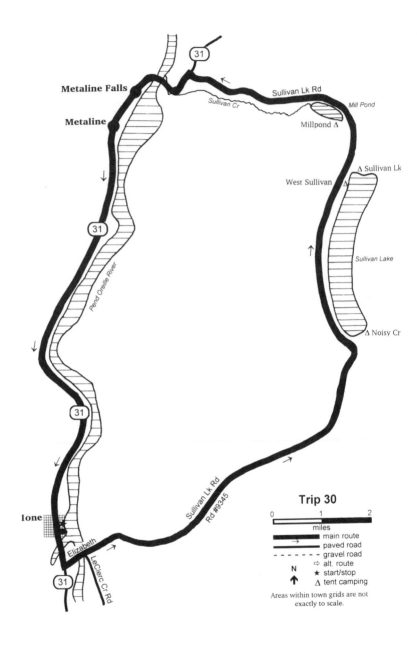

31

Metaline Falls

Metaline

Sullivan Lk Rd

Sullivan Cr

Mill Pond

Millpond △

△ Sullivan Lk

West Sullivan △

Sullivan Lake

31

Pend Oreille River

△ Noisy Cr

31

Trip 30

Sullivan Lk Rd

Rd #9345

0	1	2

miles

main route

→ paved road

- - - gravel road

⇨ alt. route

N ★ start/stop

↑ △ tent camping

Areas within town grids are not exactly to scale.

Ione

Elizabeth

LeClerc Cr Rd

31

14.0: Road 22 intersects from the right.

14.4: Reach the *Sullivan Lake Trading Post*, a seasonal store.

14.9: *Millpond Campground* entry road intersects from the left.

18.7: **Turn left** onto Highway 31 and begin a steep, winding descent. ***Caution:*** several hairpin curves.

19.8: Post Office Village Road intersects from the right.

20.6: Enter Metaline Falls—*restaurants, grocery store, motels.*

21.0: Cross the Pend Oreille River.

22.3: Enter Metaline.

24.2: A roadside park with a picnic table is to the right.

27.5: Box Canyon Dam entry road intersects from the left. A half mile later, reach Box Canyon viewpoint.

31.0: In Ione, **turn left** at milepost 4 and return to the park.

Union Flat Creek Valley (trip 38)

Stops in turn-of-the-century towns are a part of the fun.
(Main Street, Rosalia)

7

Whitman County

The rolling wheat fields of the Palouse, the foothills of the Clear-water Mountains of Idaho, the Palouse River, and centuries-old farming towns are dominant features of Whitman County. The following routes will allow you to experience them all.

Considerable flexibility is built into many of the loops: alternate routes, short cuts, and adjacent trips allow you to tailor the trip to your own needs and desires.

For the most part, the back roads of Whitman County are very lightly traveled—you'll have the road to yourself for long stretches of time. However, during key agricultural seasons such as planting and harvesting, in addition to the occasional pickup truck or lost vacationer, you'll be sharing the road with farm vehicles on their way to the next field or hauling the day's harvest to the scales or storage facility.

Trips:

31: Rosalia - Pine City - Pine Creek
32: Rosalia - Oakesdale
33: Oakesdale - Farmington
34: Garfield - Farmington
35: Palouse - Eden Valley
36: Albion - Pullman
37: St. John - Palouse Basin - Endicott
38: Colfax - Union Flat Creek Valley
39: Colfax Fairgrounds - Dusty
40: Lacrosse - Hay

31. Rosalia - Pine City - Pine Creek

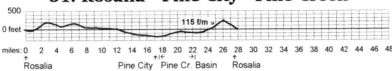

Miles: 28-44. This loop's beginning on busy Highway 195 highlights the contrast between back-road cycling and highway cycling. However, after turning onto Old Thornton Highway two miles later, you'll once again hear crickets and birds instead of cars and truck. Along Thorn Creek Road, wetlands are inhabited by red-wing blackbirds, herons, and other marsh dwellers. You'll enjoy more of the same, but on a larger scale, along Pine Creek Road, where the scent of Ponderosa Pine fills the air. Although there is a small park in Malden with a picnic table and water, there are no services en route.

Food/lodging/camping: *Rosalia*: two cafes (**509**-523-4301, 523-4201). No services en route. Closest lodging is in Steptoe (397-3195), 17 miles south of Rosalia on Highway 195.

Starting point: Rosalia is located 31 miles south of Spokane, just off Highway 195. Heading south on Highway 195, just north of Rosalia, turn right onto Whitman and follow it to the south end of town. Just before you get to the high school, turn right onto 9th Street and go one block to the city park.

    0: Return to Whitman (the main drag) and **turn right**.

  0.5: Pine City-Malden Road intersects from the right.

  1.7: **Turn right** onto the southbound on-ramp of Highway 195. Although this highway is busy, the shoulder is smooth and wide.

  3.8: Immediately past the *rest stop,* turn right onto Old Thornton Highway. The concrete pavement is rough at times, but traffic is extremely light as you make your way through wheat fields.

  7.8: **Turn right** onto Thorn Creek Road. Traffic is extremely light.

        Alt. route: To trade the level, pleasant ride along Thorn Creek for 21+ miles through hilly wheat fields, continue on Old Thornton Highway for another 2 miles to Highway 195. Turn right onto Highway 195, go 1.5 miles, and turn right onto Barnes Cut-off Road (the first paved road to the right). In another 1.2 miles, bear left onto Sunset Road. Follow

Sunset Road for approximately 11 miles and turn right onto Pine City Road (the next paved road you come to). Follow Pine City Road for about 6 miles to the junction with Thorn Creek Road (the next paved road to the right), where you rejoin the main route at the 16.2-mile mark.

16.2: **Turn right** onto Pine City-Malden Road. Traffic picks up some, but remains quite light as you move into pine-covered hills.

17.1: Enter the community of Pine City—no services.

17.4: **Bear right** where Texas Ferry Road intersects from the left. Begin a fairly level stretch through Pine Creek Basin.

20.3: **Bear right** where Wells Road intersects from the left.

20.6: Enter the community of Malden—no services.

20.7: Reach a park on the left, which has a picnic table and *water*.

22.2: After two crossings over Pine Creek, the trees become sparse as you enter an area of sagebrush and rolling wheat fields.

26.3: Reach the peak of a moderate, 2-mile climb and begin the steep, mile-long roll down the other side.

26.9: **Turn left** onto Rosalia Road (Business 195).

27.5: In Rosalia, **turn left** onto 9th Street and return to the park.

32. Rosalia - Oakesdale

Miles: 26. After a rather rambunctious start, this route mellows and becomes a gentle up-and-down trip through rolling wheat fields, complete with fantastic views of the mountains to the east. Just past the half-way point, Oakesdale—with a large, shady city park—provides a pleasant rest stop. Except for a 4-mile section of Highway 27, where volume is still fairly light, you'll encounter little traffic.

Food/lodging/camping: *Rosalia:* see trip 31. *Oakesdale:* small grocery store.

Starting point: see trip 31.

0: From the park, return to Whitman and **turn left**.

0.2: **Turn right** onto 7th Street, following signs for Memorial Field. One block later **bear right** onto 8th and continue up a short but steep hill.

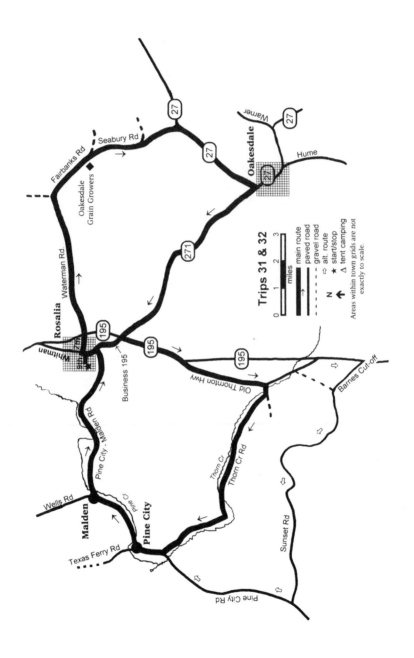

0.8: After crossing over Highway 195, the road you're on becomes Waterman Road. Traffic is very light. In another mile you'll get great views of the mountains to the east behind the rolling wheat fields.

6.6: **Bear right** onto Fairbanks Road, staying with the pavement. Traffic is extremely light as you make your way through the deserted wheat fields.

8.8: **Turn right** onto Seabury Road, just after passing the Oakesdale Grain Growers storage facility.

12.5: **Bear right** onto Highway 27, where you'll find a narrow shoulder and a moderate increase in traffic for the next 4 miles.

16.3: **Bear right** onto Highway 271, where the shoulder is come-and-go, but traffic is very light. Continue through rolling wheat fields.

Side trip: continue straight for a half mile to Oakesdale.

24.9: Cross over Highway 195 and proceed straight ahead onto Business 195.

26.7: In Rosalia, **turn left** onto 9th and return to the park.

33. Oakesdale - Farmington

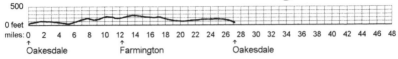

Miles: 27. This easy loop through the pea and wheat fields of the eastern-most reaches of Whitman County is ideal for those looking for a fairly long but level ride. A cafe and shady city park make Farmington an ideal place for a rest stop near the halfway point. On the way, you'll get open views of the mountains to the east. There are no significant hills on the entire route, and traffic is very light except the 8 miles on Highway 27, where traffic remains very tolerable.

Food/lodging/camping: no lodging on route. Closest lodging is in Steptoe (**509**-397-3195), 15 miles southwest of Oakesdale. *Oakesdale*: one restaurant—not in business at time of survey, grocery store. *Farmington*: one cafe (287-2015).

Starting point: Oakesdale is located 48 miles south of Spokane on Highway 27. From Highway 195, two miles south of Rosalia, take Highway 271 ten miles southeast to Oakesdale. Just north of Oakesdale, turn right onto Highway 27. In town, turn right onto Steptoe Avenue and proceed to 2nd, where you'll find the city park.

- 0: From the park, **turn left** onto Steptoe Avenue, cross 1st Street, and follow the signs for Highway 27 southbound. In .1 miles, the road bears right, passes a series of grain-storage buildings, and becomes southbound Highway 27. Traffic is light.
- 0.7: **Bear left**, staying with Highway 27 where Hume Road (unmarked) intersects from the right.
- 2.3: Warner Road intersects from the left.
- 5.5: Enter the community of Belmont, which consists of 4 or 5 houses and a couple of grain storage buildings.
- 7.0: **Turn left** onto Farmington Road, where traffic is very light.
- 12.3: Enter the town of Farmington, which has a small cafe and a very pleasant park—*water,* shade, and tables.
- 12.7: **Turn left** onto Farmington Road (3rd Avenue), following the signs to Seltice and Tekoa.
- 18.0: **Turn left** onto Seltice Road At the stop sign, **turn left** again onto unmarked Warner Road, where traffic is extremely light.
- 24.8: **Turn right** onto unmarked Highway 27.

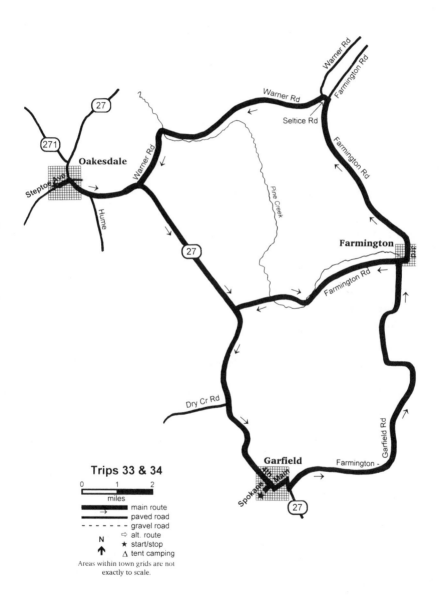

Trips 33 & 34

0   1   2
miles

━━━ main route
→ paved road
- - - - gravel road
⇨ alt. route
N   ★ start/stop
↑   △ tent camping

Areas within town grids are not
exactly to scale.

27.1: In Oakesdale, **cross** 1st Street where Highway 27 swings to the right. You are now on Steptoe Avenue. The park is one block ahead on your right.

34. Garfield - Farmington

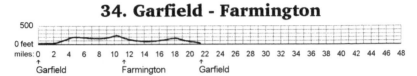

Miles: 21. This short, scenic loop is a virtually level cruise through the wheat fields of the Palouse, with the mountains to the east providing a scenic backdrop. Except for a 5-mile stretch of Highway 27, you'll have the road to yourself most of the time. At the halfway point, Farmington offers a park and a cafe.

Food/lodging/camping: No lodging en route. Closest lodging is in Steptoe (**509**-397-3195), 12 miles east. *Garfield*: tavern (635-1602), cafe (635-1412), small grocery store. *Farmington*: cafe (287-2015).

Starting point: Garfield is located approximately 60 miles south of Spokane on Highway 27. From southbound Highway 27, take a right on Spokane Street. Go one block to the city park.

    0: Return to Highway 27 (Fourth Street) and **turn right**. A couple of blocks later, **bear left** to stay on Highway 27.

  0.6: **Bear right** after crossing the RR tracks.

  0.7: **Turn left** onto Farmington-Garfield Road (unmarked). Landmark: immediately after turning, you'll pass a power substation on the left. This narrow, scenic road offers regular views of the mountains to the east. Traffic is extremely light.

 11.3: **Turn left** onto Farmington Road, heading toward Highway 27. That's Steptoe Butte (3500 ft.) dead ahead. Traffic is very light.
       Side trip: turn right and go a quarter mile into the town of Farmington—*cafe* and shady city park.

 16.3: **Turn left** onto Highway 27, where you'll find a foot-wide shoulder and light traffic.

 19.1: Dry Creek Road intersects from the right.

 21.5: In the town of Garfield, **turn right** onto Spokane Street and return to the city park.

35. Palouse - Eden Valley

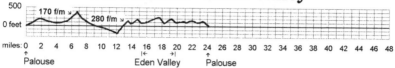

Miles: 24. The first portion of this classic cycling loop begins in the sleepy town of Palouse with a moderate climb out of town. Near the 2-mile point, you begin a fairly level two miles before another, steeper climb peaks a the 7-mile point, then sends you on a 5-mile descent to Highway 272. The second half begins with the steepest climb of the trip. After reaching the peak, a succession of smaller hills has you going up one moment and down the next. Scenery is top-notch; Kamiak Butte, Eden Valley, and the Palouse Range are notable highlights.

Food/lodging/camping: *Palouse*: no lodging (see trip 38 for lodging in Colfax), restaurant (**509**-878-1208) tavern (878-1919), small grocery store. No services en route.

Starting point: Palouse is located approximately 70 miles south of Spokane on Highway 27. From southbound Highway 27, proceed to the center of town and turn right at the signs for the city park. Go four blocks to the park.

0: Return to Highway 27, turn right, and cross the Palouse River. Begin climbing through rolling wheat fields as views of the mountains to the east keep you company.

1.8: Kamiak Butte comes into view as you reach the crest.

3.4: **Turn right** onto Clear Creek Road, where traffic decreases. As you continue through rolling wheat fields, Kamiak Butte is in full view to the immediate left.

3.9: Fugate Road (gravel), leading to a wildlife viewing area, intersects from the left. A fairly steep grade lies ahead.

6.9: Reach the crest of the hill and begin a five-mile descent, gliding into pine-wooded fields in the draw irrigated by Clear Creek.

12.3: **Turn right** onto Highway 272 (unmarked) and begin a steep climb. A couple miles (and a few hills) later, you'll be in scenic Eden Valley.

23.0: Cross the Palouse River and a *very rough RR crossing*.

23.6: **Turn right** onto Highway 27.

23.8: **Turn right** at the flashing light, following the sign to the park.

107

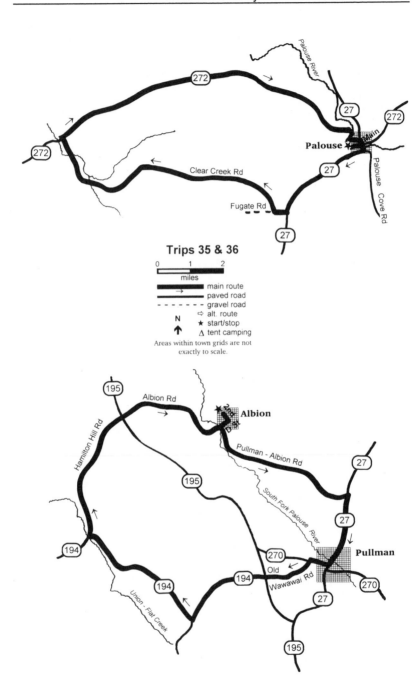

Trips 35 & 36

0   1   2
miles

━━━━━ main route
─────→ paved road
─ ─ ─ ─ gravel road
⇨ alt. route
★ start/stop
△ tent camping

N ↑

Areas within town grids are not
exactly to scale.

36. Albion - Pullman

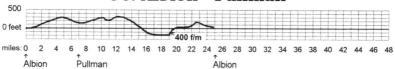

Miles: 25. Beginning with an easy, 4-mile climb, this first third of this route is comprised of wheat fields. In Pullman—home of WSU—a bike path and sidewalk where bikes are permitted make the downtown stretch of Highway 27 quite tolerable. After a moderate, 4-mile climb out of Pullman, a long descent takes you to an oasis (compliments of Union-Flat Creek) in the midst of the wheat fields, where you'll find woodlands, lush grazing lands, and wetlands. A steep, mile-long climb out sends you back to the rolling fields and intermittent views of the mountains to the east. Except for 3 miles on Highway 27 and Highway 270 in Pullman, traffic is very light the entire way. To start the loop in Pullman, begin at Sunnyside Park (8.5-mile mark).

Food/lodging/camping: *Albion:* no services. *Pullman:* all services.

Starting point: About 7 miles south of Colfax (on Highway 195) turn east onto Albion Road. In 5 miles you'll come to a stop sign at a T. Continue straight onto D Street. Two blocks later, turn left onto 2nd Street (unmarked) and go one block to the park.

   0: From the park, head back to D Street and **turn right**.

 0.2: **Turn left** at the stop sign onto Front Street (unmarked), following signs for Pullman.

 5.3: **Turn right** onto busy Highway 27, where there is a two-foot shoulder. Shortly, a paved bike path will get you off the highway.

 7.5: **Turn right** onto Highway 270.

 8.2: **Turn left** onto Old Wawawai Road (Highway 194), following signs to Wawawai and Almota. Traffic becomes very light.

 8.5: Reach Sunnyside Park.

 9.9: Cross Highway 195.

12.7: **Bear right**, staying with Highway 194.

14.3: Trees appear in the scenery as you descend to the green woodlands and fields of Union-Flat Creek.

17.1: **Turn right** onto Hamilton Hill Road at the Almota Elevator silos.

18.7: Begin a steep climb that moderates in a half mile and, at the top, offers panoramic views of the mountains to the east.

21.4: **Cross Highway 195** onto Albion Road.

25.1: At the stop sign, **continue straight** onto D Street. Two blocks later **turn left** on 2nd (unmarked) and return to the park.

37. St. John - Palouse Basin - Endicott

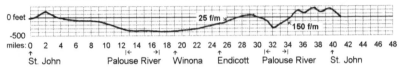

Miles: 40. All-but-deserted roads, two passes through a rocky river basin, and well-placed stops make this a terrific loop. The first descent and climb out from the lush, irrigated Palouse Basin is so gentle you'll hardly notice it. However, the second time through begins with a fairly steep 3-mile roll into the basin, a steeper, 3-mile climb out, and a couple 200-foot hills to follow. If you like to do your hill climbing during the first half of a trip, ride the route in the reverse direction. When you're not in the basin, the terrain is mostly wheat fields and sagebrush.

Food/lodging/camping: No lodging on route. Closest lodging is in Steptoe, 14 miles east. *St. John*: cafe (509-648-3759), 2 small grocery stores. *Endicott*: cafe was out of business at time of survey, small grocery store, park.

Starting point: In Steptoe (fifty miles south of Spokane on Highway 195) take Highway 23 northbound. Fifteen miles later, in the center of St. John, turn left where signs indicate Endicott is 15 miles south. Four blocks later, turn right on State Street and go one block to the park.

0: Head east on State Street. One block later, at the stop sign, **turn left** onto the unmarked street.

0.2: **Turn left** onto unmarked Highway 23 at the next stop sign.

0.4: **Bear left** onto Lancaster Road/Front Street (unmarked) and cross a small creek. Traffic is extremely light.

0.7: Pass the St. John Golf and Country Club and begin a one-mile, moderate climb. Watch for a ***rough RR crossing*** in two miles.

6.8: Enter the community of Lancaster—no services.

12.6: The gradual descent into the Palouse Basin is nearly over.

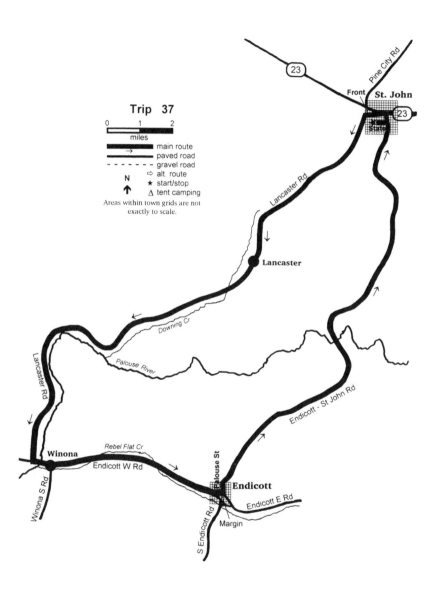

Trip 37

0   1   2
miles

━━━ main route
→
──── paved road
- - - - - gravel road
⇨ alt. route
N
★ start/stop
↑ △ tent camping

Areas within town grids are not
exactly to scale.

18.8: **Turn left** onto Endicott Road and cross the Palouse River. Enter the tiny community of Winona—no services. At the far end of town, after crossing the RR tracks, there is a shaded *picnic area* with a table and *water.*

24.9: In Endicott, **turn left** onto Margin Street (unmarked) just after passing the high school, following the sign to St. John. **Turn left** again one block later onto Palouse (unmarked), which becomes Endicott-Saint John Road beyond the city limits. Landmark: pass a cemetery in a quarter mile.

> *Side trip 1:* Instead of turning left onto Margin, continue straight into town, where you will find a small *grocery store* and a service station with *restrooms.*

> *Side trip 2:* After turning left onto Margin, continue straight to the city park where you'll find picnic tables, but no water or restrooms.

29.0: See the top of Steptoe Butte in the distance to the east.

31.6: Cross the Palouse River as you near the bottom of the descent. The fairly steep climb out begins almost immediately.

35.0: Reach the top of the the basin and return to the wheat fields. A couple of 200-foot ups and downs lie ahead.

39.8: In St. John, **turn left** on State Street and return to the park.

38. Colfax - Union Flat Creek Valley

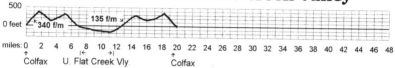

Miles: 21-64. This trip to Union Flat Creek begins with a bang: a steep, 1.5-mile climb out of the Colfax Valley. After cresting a second hill, a 2-mile roll takes you into Union Flat Creek Valley for a pleasant, nearly level, 4-mile cruise along the creek. In the valley, the topography changes from wheat fields to rugged, rocky scabland punctuated with conifers and wetlands irrigated by the creek. After a moderate climb out, hilly wheat fields monopolize the scenery the rest of the way. To add 30 to 42 miles, connect to trip 37 (details below).

Food/lodging/camping: *Colfax:* Siesta Motel (509-397-3417), several restaurants services. No services en route.

Starting point: Colfax is located 58 miles south of Spokane on Highway 195. Follow 195 almost all the way to the south end of town. At the Siesta Motel, take a right onto Thorn Street and go two blocks to Hamilton Park.

0: Head back toward Highway 195 on Thorn, go one block, and **turn right** onto Lake Street. One block later, **turn left** onto Wawawai Street.

0.1: **Turn right** onto Main Street and begin a moderate incline.

0.3: **Bear right** onto Fairview Street at the yield sign. The climb steepens and then moderates a quarter mile later.

1.1: Airport Road intersects from the right as the road you're on becomes Almota Road. Traffic is very light as you move through open, hilly wheat fields. In another quarter mile, you'll begin a 1.5-mile descent down the other side of the hill. This is only a brief respite before the next 200-foot climb. However, after cresting that hill, you'll make a 2-mile descent to Wilson Creek.

6.8: **Turn right** onto Sommers Road (on some maps this is shown as Wilcox Road). Traffic is extremely light. The topography in the valley changes to rockier sagebrush land with scattered conifers and wetlands.

11.1: **Turn right** onto Highway 26. Traffic is moderate and the shoulder is generous as you begin a 3-mile, moderate climb back into hilly wheat fields.

113

15.3: **Turn right** onto Colfax Airport Road as you approach the fairgrounds. Traffic decreases.

> *Alt. route*: For a smoother, more gradual descent into Colfax (the trade-off is heavier traffic), continue straight on Highway 26 for another 4 miles. Turn right onto Highway 195 and follow the starting-point instructions to return to Hamilton Park.

> *Side trip*: To add 30-42 miles to the trip, turn left on Fairgrounds Road and begin trip 37.

18.5: **Turn left** onto Almota Road. The steep coast back into Colfax is rather frustrating, requiring braking to stay within the 25-mph speed limit as the road passes through a residential area.

19.2: **Turn left** onto Lake Street. Three blocks later, **turn left** onto Thorn Street.

39. Colfax Fairgrounds - Dusty

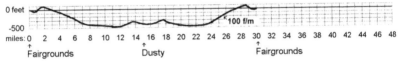

Miles: 0 2 4 6 8 10 12 14 16 18 20 22 24 26 28 30 32 34 36 38 40 42 44 46 48
Fairgrounds   Dusty   Fairgrounds

Miles: 30-43. This scenic out-and-back trip (which can be turned into a loop by returning on Highway 26) runs through a charming, wooded creek valley. Chances are you'll see deer and other wildlife. The descent and climb out are quite tame. Traffic is very light the entire way. In Dusty you'll find a cafe, and the starting point of an optional, 12-mile loop through rolling wheat fields.

Food/lodging/camping: *Colfax*: Siesta Motel (**509**-397-3417), Boyer Park Campground (397-3208), several restaurants. *Dusty*: cafe (549-3528). *Fairgrounds*: tent camping (397-3712).

Starting point: Just north of Colfax, turn west onto Highway 26. Four miles later, turn right onto Fairgrounds Road and park along the shoulder in front of the fairgrounds fence.

0: Head north on Fairgrounds Road.

0.4: **Turn left** onto Endicott Road.

0.9: **Turn left** onto McNeilly Road and begin a gradual climb through wheat fields. After cresting this hill in another half mile, you'll begin the long, pleasant descent into the valley.

6.6: **Bear right** to stay on McNeilly Road where Union-Flat Creek Road intersects from the left.

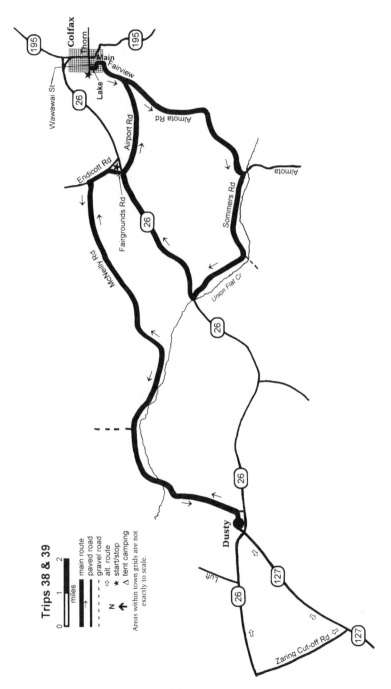

Trips 38 & 39

miles
0 1 2

main route
paved road
gravel road
alt. route
★ start/stop
△ tent camping

N

Areas within town grids are not exactly to scale.

14.6: **Turn right** onto an unmarked paved road, just before reaching the junction with Highway 26. A *rest area* with *outhouses* is on the right-hand side.

15.1: Reach the town of Dusty, which is the turn-around point unless you're taking the optional loop. After heading back on the road you came in on, turn left onto Young Road (also called Mader Road) at the rest stop. Then, retrace the route all the way back to Endicott Road. Turn right onto Endicott Road, and about a half mile later, turn right again onto Fairgrounds Road (unmarked).

> *Side trip*: To add 12 miles through rolling wheat fields, proceed past the cafe, cross Highway 26, and head south on Highway 127, which is smooth and flat and has a wide shoulder. Traffic is moderate. In about 4.5 miles, turn right onto Zaring Cutoff Road. In another 3 miles, turn right onto Highway 26 (unmarked), which has a wide shoulder and moderate traffic. In another 5 miles, turn left onto Dusty Road and return to the Dusty Cafe.
>
> *Alt. route*: Return to the fairgrounds via Highway 26.

40. Lacrosse - Hay

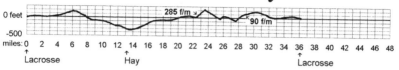

Miles: 36. This loop through the hilly, multi-colored wheat fields of the Palouse begins in the small town of Lacrosse, makes a gradual descent to Alkali Flat Creek and the tiny community of Hay, climbs steadily back out, and then cuts across hilly Church Hill Road before returning to Lacrosse. If you're looking for solitude and an opportunity to examine the Palouse wheat fields from every possible angle, this is the trip. The patchwork of browns, yellows and greens extending as far as the eye can see is a wonder to behold.

Food/lodging/camping: No lodging on route. Closest lodging is in Washtucna (20 miles west) or Colfax (25 miles east). *Lacrosse:* no lodging, cafe (509-549-3560).

Starting point: From Highway 26, turn north on Scott Road and follow it into town, where the road is renamed Main Avenue. At the far end of town, find the city park.

0: From the park, return to town on Main and continue on to Highway 26.

2.0: **Turn left** onto Highway 26, where you'll find moderate traffic and a wide shoulder.

3.6: **Turn right** onto Hay-Lacrosse Road. Traffic is extremely light.

8.8: **Turn right** to stay on Hay-Lacrosse, where Selbu Church Road intersects from the left.

10.7: The view opens up as you enter a basin irrigated by Mud Flat Creek. The wheat fields carved into the hillsides give the land a sculptured look.

13.2: **Turn left** onto Big Alkali Road (unmarked) and continue straight as Little Goose Dam Road intersects from the right.

22.7: **Turn left** onto Church Hill Road and begin a steep, one-mile ascent. At the top, you'll be rewarded with a panoramic view.

27.2: **Turn right** onto Hay-Lacrosse Road.

32.4: **Turn left** onto Highway 26.

34.0: **Turn right** onto Scott Road.

35.5: Enter Lacrosse and return to the park.

117

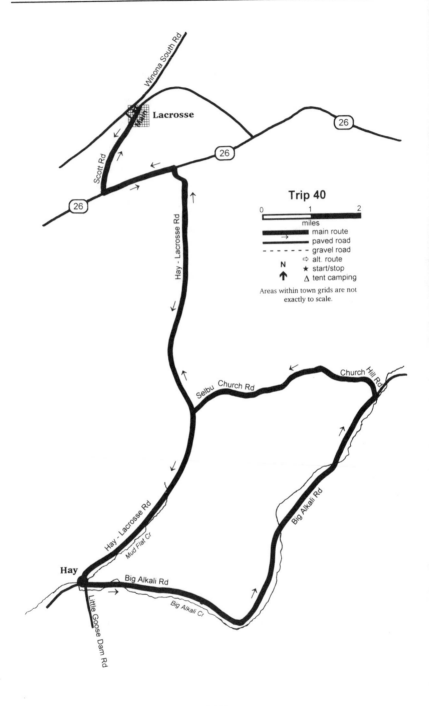

Trip 40

0   1   2
miles
main route
→ paved road
- - - - gravel road
⇨ alt. route
N   ★ start/stop
↑   △ tent camping

Areas within town grids are not
exactly to scale.

Lacrosse

Winona South Rd

Scott Rd

26

26

26

Hay - Lacrosse Rd

Selbu Church Rd

Church Hill Rd

Big Alkali Rd

Hay - Lacrosse Rd

Mud Flat Cr

Hay

Big Alkali Rd

Little Goose Dam Rd

Big Alkali Cr

8

Bike Vacations and Tours

Trips can be combined both for extensive tours on a bicycle alone or for *car-hop* tours. When planning either type of tour, a restricting factor is the location of restaurants, motels, and campgrounds. Consult the trip-connector maps for an overview of locations where lodging can be found. You will find contact information for motels, campgrounds, and restaurants included in the trip descriptions in previous chapters. Make motel and campground reservations well in advance of your trip and confirm operating hours of cafes in small towns.

Car-hop tours allow cyclists to ride through a wide variety of scenery over a period of several days without the added weight of sleeping bags, tents, and other equipment. The concept is simple: determine which trips you want to take, consult the trip-connector maps to find the nearest lodging for each trip, and decide upon a logical progression for the tour. At the end of each day, load your bike back onto your vehicle and head for the next destination. From Cheney, Davenport, Colville, and Steptoe, the starting points of a number of trips are within a few miles. One can lodge for several days in these towns, bike a different route every day, and never drive more than an hour to get to a starting point.

Car-hop tours can be custom tailored to your ability level. They offer an excellent introduction to long-distance cycling, providing beginners with an opportunity to get a feel for bike touring before committing to the demands of several days of cycling with heavy packs. In addition, car-hop tours can be designed as vacations for families with older children. Cycling the loops can be combined with camping, fishing, hiking, swimming and other activities. Contact local chambers of commerce for more details on recreational opportunities in the areas you're planning to visit.

119

Below is a five-day car-hop tour that includes several scenic loops ranging from relatively easy to moderately difficult. This tour takes you through the majority of the region over the five-day period.

Day 1: Begin with a trip through the scablands of Lincoln County with trip 18 or 14. Drive to Cheney at the end of the day.

Day 2: From Cheney, do one or a combination of the two Turnbull Wildlife Refuge trips or trip 4 out of Medical Lake.

Day 3: After another night in Cheney, drive to Fairfield and take trip 10, possibly combined with trip 9 if you're up to it. Drive to Chewelah after the day's ride, stopping at one of Spokane's many bike shops for parts, repairs, or supplies you may need.

Day 4: From Chewelah, do trip 23 or drive to Addy for trips 24 or 25. Drive to Ione after the day's ride.

Day 5: End the tour in style with the scenic Sullivan Lake loop through the Colville National Forest (trip 30).

Tours can be designed specifically for beginning cyclists interested in putting in some miles without over exerting themselves. For example, trips 2, 5, 13, 31, 34, and 39 encompass a wide variety of scenery with a minimum of significant hills.

When planning a traditional cycling tour, where your bike will be your only mode of transportation for the entire trip, keep in mind that some of the connecting roads are quite challenging. They also vary greatly in terms of traffic level and shoulder width. In the northern half of the region, the connecting roads between Highway 395 and Highway 25 are steep and winding (Cedonia-Addy Road is the best bet). Highway 395 has fairly wide shoulders from Spokane to Kettle Falls. Between Kettle Falls and Barstow, shoulders are quite narrow. Beyond Barstow, shoulders are virtually nonexistent, and heavy semi-truck traffic en route to Canada intensifies the already perilous situation—this section of 395 should be avoided entirely.

If you're willing to go a little out of the way—and if you're not, it's time to take a hard look at your cycling psychology—Highway 395 can be largely avoided from Spokane to Kettle Falls by utilizing the back roads indicated on the maps in this chapter. The section between Garden Spot Road and Hafer Road can be dodged by taking Highway 292 over to Highway 231 and then catching Long Prairie Road up to Farm To Market Road on the west side of trip 23. In addition to avoiding heavy traffic on 395, you'll pass through some of the most beautiful country in the region.

Highway 20 (Tiger Pass) is the only paved route from the Colville Valley to the Pend Oreille Valley. Of necessity, it is a common route for touring cyclists. From Colville to the summit, the shoulders are at least adequate in most places. From the summit to Tiger, shoulders are very narrow. Use extra caution on this steep, winding pass.

Throughout the northern part of the region, watch for logging trucks running back and forth from the forests to the mills.

In the northeastern quadrant, the road from Elk to trip 22 is very steep, shoulderless, and narrow through Camden Gap—use extreme caution. LeClerc Road, running 50 miles from Newport to Ione is relatively flat as well as very scenic—a textbook example of an ideal cycling road.

In the southwestern quadrant, Highway 272 from Colfax to trip 35 is very steep and narrow. While Highway 195 can be quite busy, there is a generous shoulder between Spokane and Pullman. From Fairfield south to Oakesdale, Highway 27 is winding and has very narrow shoulders; the situation improves south of Oakesdale. Highway 23 from Sprague to Steptoe has narrow shoulders. Highway 26 has a good shoulder and only moderate traffic all the way through Whitman County and Adams County.

All the connecting roads in the southwestern quadrant are quite good for cycling. Except for I-90 and Highway 395, even the highways are lightly traveled—rated by the state Department of Transportation at less than 2,000 cars per day. Highway 261 between Ritzville and Ralston has sections where the roadway is winding and shoulders are narrow; the situation clears up significantly south of Ralston. Most of the connecting roads in this part of the region are free of long, steep hills; however, many constantly move up and down over rolling hills as they make their way through scabland and wheat fields, racking up fairly significant cumulative elevation gains.

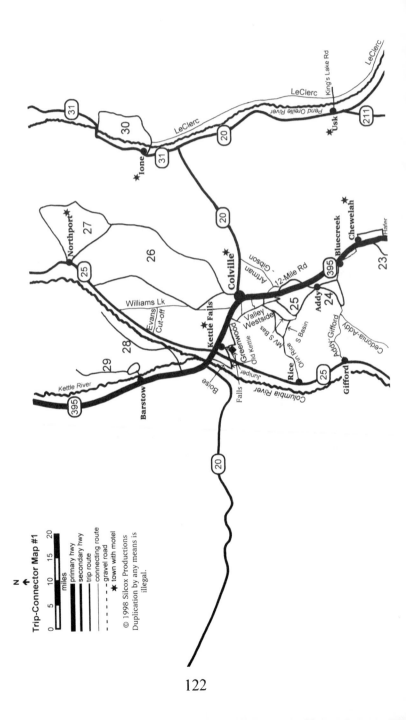

Trip-Connector Map #1

miles
0 5 10 15 20

primary hwy
secondary hwy
trip route
connecting route
gravel road
★ town with motel

© 1998 Silcox Productions
Duplication by any means is
illegal.

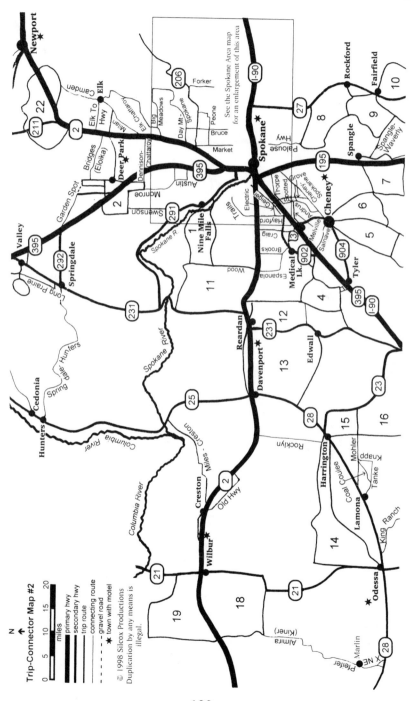

Trip-Connector Map #2

0 5 10 15 20
miles
primary hwy
secondary hwy
trip route
connecting route
gravel road
★ town with motel

© 1998 Silcox Productions
Duplication by any means is
illegal.

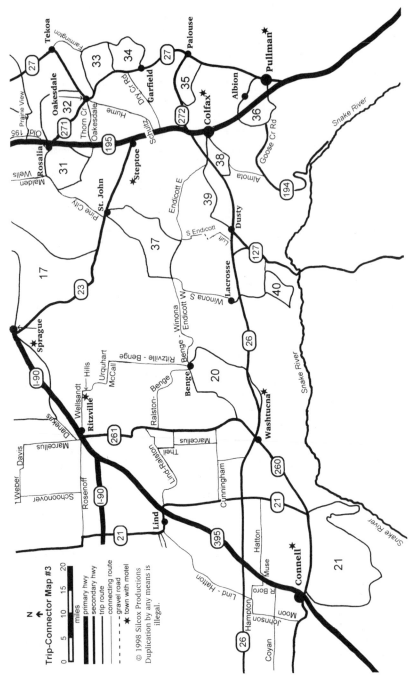

Trip-Connector Map #3

miles
0 5 10 15 20

N ←

primary hwy
secondary hwy
trip route
connecting route
★ town with motel

© 1998 Silcox Productions
Duplication by any means is
illegal.

Appendix

Spokane Area Visitor Information Center
201 W. Main
Spokane WA 99201
509-747-3230, 800-248-3230
Free maps of Spokane and other resources

Northwest Map & Travel Book Center
525 W Sprague
Spokane WA
509-455-6981

Spokane Bicycle Club
P O Box 62
Spokane WA 99210
509-325-1171
www.iea.com/~rlee/sbc
Recreational rides and events

League of American Bicyclists
1612 K Street NW
Suite 401
(202) 822-1333
http://www.bikeleague.org

Friends of the Centennial Trail
P O Box 351
Spokane WA 99210
509-624-7188
Maps and information

Spokane Bicycling Coordinator
Dept. of Planning
3rd Floor Municipal Bldg.
808 W Spokane Falls St.
Spokane WA
509-625-6144

Washington State Dept. of Transportation
Bicycle Pedestrian Program Manager
P O Box 47393
Olympia WA 98504-7393
350-705-7258

Baddlands Cycling Club
Spokane WA
509-235-3880
Racing club

The Bicycle Paper
1535 11th Ave.
Seattle WA 98105
Covers cycling events in Washington and Oregon

Oregon Cycling Magazine
544 W 1st Ave
Eugene OR 97401
Covers cycling events and issues

Washington State Lodging and Travel Guide
1-800-544-1800

Add your name to the Silcox Productions Mailing List!

Get information on new Eastern Washington maps, guides and other publications.

Send you name and address to:

Silcox Productions
P O Box 1407
Orient WA 99160
509-684-8287
dheflick@plix.com

Additional copies of this book are available direct from Silcox Productions for $13.95 plus $2.00 shipping and handling.

Add your name to the Silcox Productions Mailing List!

Get information on new Eastern Washington maps, guides and other publications.

Send your name and address to:

Silcox Productions
P O Box 1407
Orient WA 99160
509-684-8287
dheflick@plix.com

Additional copies of this book are available direct from Silcox Productions for $13.95 plus $2.00 shipping and handling.